SEEDTIME III

W0010461

Philippe Jaccottet

SEEDTIME III

NOTEBOOKS
1995–1998

Translated by Tess Lewis

LONDON NEW YORK CALCUTTA

swiss arts council
prᴏhelvetia

This publication has
been supported by a
grant from Pro Helvetia,
Swiss Arts Council,
which funds the work's
translation costs.

**PAP
TAGORE**
www.bibliofrance.in

This work is published
with the support of the
Publication Assistance
Pogrammes of the
Institut Français, which
partially funds the
work's production costs.

Seagull Books, 2021

Originally published in French as Philippe Jaccottet,
Carnets 1995–1998 (*La Semaison III*)
© Editions Gallimard, Paris, 2001

First published in English translation by Seagull Books, 2021
English translation © Tess Lewis, 2021

ISBN   978 0 8574 2 848 6

British Library Cataloguing-in-Publication Data
A catalogue record for this book is available from the
British Library.

Typeset by Seagull Books, Calcutta, India
Printed and bound by Versa Press, Peoria, IL, USA

CONTENTS

Semaison: The natural dispersion of a plant's seeds.

Littré

1995

Magnelli collection at Beaubourg. Alongside a few sober and somewhat cold canvases by this painter there is a series of African sculptures he had acquired, a few of which are very impressive; but looking at them, it's impossible to forget they were sacred objects that do not belong in a museum. Reduced to form as they were by the painters who chose them back then, they're almost completely bereft of their meaning. Whatever our views, we cannot deny that the more or less elaborate use to which modern artists put them inevitably strikes a more or less hollow sound.

Loss of meaning: when dervishes begin whirling on a stage, it is without question the beginning of their degradation—ecstasy 'as spectacle' is perforce half-feigned. Think of the very latest fairground sideshows: 'Step right up! For the very low price of five francs, you can see a saint in a swoon, an ascetic levitating before your eyes!'

This is why one should not ape any of it.

❧

1

Returning to Goethe while preparing my *Second Seed-time* for press, I leaf, dismayed, through the French translation of the *West-Eastern Divan* published in the Poésie / Gallimard series. Who on earth was it that wrote one of the most beautiful poems in this book was the posthumous '*Nicht mehr auf Seidenblatt*'? Walter Benjamin? In any case, he quotes a verse in one of the stories in the collection *Rastelli's Story*.[1] All the same, I hesitate to quote the poem, not having come up with a better version than Henri Lichtenberger's.

> I no longer write on pages of silk
> Symmetrical rhymes;
> I no longer border them
> With leaves of gold;
> Inscribed in shifting sands,
> The wind sweeps them away, though their power holds,
> To the centre of the earth
> In thrall to the ground.
> And the wanderer, the lover
> Will come. Were he to step foot
> On this spot, his every limb would tremble.
> 'Here! A lover loved before me,
> Was it tender Majnun?
> Mighty Farhad? Steadfast Jamil?
> Or another of those thousands
> Happy-unhappy ones?
> He loved! I love as he did,

I can sense him here.'[2]
Yet you, Suleika, you sleep on the soft pillow
I prepared and adorned for you.
You too are roused by trembling in your limbs:
'It is he, Hatem, who calls me.
And I call you, Hatem, Hatem!'

Nearly transparent haze—white clouds or Alps suspended in the sky's pallid blue above the horizon.

Below the Rocher des Fées you can hear the sound of a hidden waterfall that changes according to the wind. Montréal-les-Sources is a vast combe in which many sources of water are, in fact, visible: dark flows of marl and sinkholes. I particularly remember that small apricot orchard against a background of pale, beige dirt. In its midst rose a house of the same shade, encircled with bare trees like so many hieroglyphs. It could have been painted by Morandi with the almost funereal undertones of marl: Grizzana during the war.

The hardening palm, bone turning to stone; like boulders surfacing in a gentle valley. We become more like rock; for a long time, the bone begins to manifest itself, to reveal its power and the way it prevails in the end. Not for ever. This is death gaining ground within us, not like a fruit as Rilke had dreamt: like a stone. As for the garment, it frays, unravels. These, at least, are certitudes you can build on; or, on the contrary, you can abandon building altogether.

MAY

Summer weather. And associated with these days, in the garden, a birdsong heard for years, from a distance, a short phrase, like the oriole's; in any case, like the oriole's song in that it resembles a call, an utterance from the other side of the world; difficult to grasp, very pure, very liquid; above all, communicating, seeming to communicate, to indicate a distance; and as a consequence this song is almost seductive and faintly mocking, like a child calling that you can't catch him or a woman, confident she is out of reach and will not be taken; at the same time, as they always do, these comparisons betray the singular reality of this song, which seems tied to beautiful weather, to the first real warmth. This song, saying calmly, perhaps even with indifference, that there is another world within our own; saying it luminously.

And here it is again, on another day in this month of May, in the pallor of the sky, as if located behind the web woven by the swifts' flight and sometimes even in the centre of their circles; this very pure, very resonant, liquescent call; two notes of different pitches or more often three; one long and two short, the middle note being the highest, although sometimes it's the first; in the visible thickening of the foliage.

Then the invisible bird falls silent; or has flown further off. The dowser bird. The water carrier. The cry of the water carrier, of the water seller in the souks; here in this leafy labyrinth.

NOVEMBER

Smoke, like an itinerant tree. Fire's floating crest.

The journey of an envoy of the Dalai Lama to the Kingdom of Lo. Rocky landscapes crossed on horseback over bumpy paths and trails. Vultures soaring over the crags. A peasant who has just bought several yaks passes by. These heavy, black-and-white beasts with the hair of their coats hanging down to the ground seem to have come from another age and, although more laden with mythology than any bull, they are nonetheless perfectly at home in these arid elevations.

The villages are barely villages, rather, accu-
mulations of stones or ruins. The villagers, short,
stooped and wrinkled, clad in dark rags such as you
only see these days on extras in films set in the Middle
Ages, rush to touch the robe of the lama coming from
India. On the occasion of this arrival, we catch a
glimpse of a celebration in one of the houses: a man
dancing or, rather, tottering clumsily, wildly, and
others seated, drinking; all this without the slightest
grace or any apparent joy. At a stage in the journey, a
lama welcomes the messenger at his home; a sickly
man, ageless, with mobile, nervous features. Hanging
from the low ceiling in a dim room, we can discern a
ghastly animal that looks more like a pale, moth-eaten
seal than one of the predatory cats. When the guest
lama suggests he recognized a snow leopard, his host
confirms his guess is correct and immediately began
mimicking the animal's bearing: how it threatens a
man—or a lamb—leaps on him, bites the nape of
his neck. He does this feverishly and with increasing
fervour as if he were an actor trained by Artaud or,
rather, something possessed.

Finally, the modest ambassador arrives within
sight of the capital—having skirted mountains resembling ancient fortresses of sand. Seen from a distance,
it is a small expanse of prairie before external walls
behind which other white or ochre walls rise slightly:
the palace and the temple. On his rather square head,

the king wears a kind of bonnet made of white wool. His features are heavy but without any hardness. For that matter, everything, the palace and the temple are of modest dimensions and rickety appearance. For a moment, I thought that Ulysses, King of Ithaca, must have received guests with no greater ceremony. But here there are the lamas' horns, sometimes so long two men are needed to carry them, pointed hats worn by some of those present, the cavernous hum of the liturgies; the vast spaces, clouds often swept away by winds we suppose extremely violent above the highest mountains on the globe. The impression we take away from these incursions into the last enclaves still unscathed by 'progress' occasionally broadcast on television is, once again, not that of having intruded into some paradise or of having glimpsed some way of life lost to us. Rather, it is one of having briefly entered the world of the epopee, the world of myths—in which it seems to us, also to us, legitimate to have imagined gods on the mountaintops and close bonds between the gods and vultures, yaks and snow leopards. In these images, so remote from those of the Dalai Lama in his comfortable office in the middle of a lush park, there was the same kind of hard, elementary, immemorial beauty as in all forms of archaic art; not more happiness, certainly not, nor more joy or grace—no grace at all—but, if we can speak in such terms, more 'truth'—or at least a greater proximity to the elementary: to bone, blood, stone, fire, water. (Funeral rites: the body is cut up in the open air for the vultures to strip it to the bones, so that nothing remains to impede the soul's path to illumination. We heard, or believed we heard, the master sharpening his knife at the edge of the torrent.)

On the way back, the Dalai Lama's messenger, who at sixty-five believed himself very old, paused at the top of a pass from which he could see, from afar, now occupied Tibet. He had multicoloured prayer flags strung up and they began to snap in the wind like the pennants you used to see—perhaps you still can— on boats anchored in large ports; he stood motionless for a long time; and, observing this homeland he knows he can never return to and praying that it would once again attain a freedom one hardly dares believe in, he began to weep behind his joined hands.

The feeling, evermore acute, of not having enough time, of haste. The sunlit leaves, increasingly rare— the way sails are furled. These last remaining leaves create a kind of fire in the rain, a fire that provides but little warmth. The creaking of branches, creaking of bones; like that of a ship's bulkheads in the ocean's cold, grey, menacing swells. How hostile these blind waters, stretching out endlessly, seemed to me by dint of their indifference! At least you can step on the swells of mountains. There, I felt surrounded by graves ready to gape, to yawn, frigid, bottomless pits; shrouds tirelessly unfolded, refolded. Forever refusing the least candle, the least cross, the least flower. Colours of steel, of iron verdigris, of ice. The least bird astray over it was like a small flame illuminating a cave. The sunlight hitting these waters became the clatter of ancient weapons, an ancient epic exhausting the eyes and the spirit.

After having seen a television documentary about Segalen with lovely material, I tried to reread *Équipée*,[3] once again without conviction. Wasn't there in Segalen another kind of Parnassian as well, a calligrapher a little too rigid, haughty, solemn—too much the 'artist'? One should reread *Stèles* before condemning him too expeditiously. Yet no matter what page you read of Claudel on China, isn't his writing vibrant and substantial in a different kind of way? In their exquisiteness, his manuscripts prefigure those of Saint-John Perse, in whom I nevertheless see greater depth and ingenuity.

What is more, it seems to me that with Segalen, you never escape that penchant for exoticism that also ruins the Gauguin's works. Did he not also succumb to the utopia of the 'noble savage' corrupted by civilization?

Vague images on the night following these notes, some almost completely faded, others certainly lost:

A man standing behind a bare table who had not written anything or planned for his near departure; it seemed to me that only the attention with which he looked at things was keeping him firmly upright, an attention which, after all, was perhaps on the contrary, just a way of blinding himself.

I also saw the thin young girl in a long, black dress, not at all funereal, in the field, standing up very straight and not saying a word as in a dream—although it was one—as distant as figures in dreams, graceful and almost absent.

'*Singing the earth's glory in order to no longer see it*': I remembered this line from 'Requiem', written almost fifty years ago, with the word 'glory', which, there is no doubt, came to me from Jouve, (who, I'll note in passing, wrote an afterword to my edition of Segalen, which is no coincidence—I distanced myself from the one as from the other for rather similar reasons.)

Would I have the right, today, a half-century later, to rewrite the line, like this for example: 'Attempting to say, to translate the light of this world to see more clearly,' to see beyond this world more clearly, to better perceive the totality of my experience? At least that's what I'd like to believe in rare moments of confidence. There will, then, be no occasion, as the moment of departure nears, to strike a pose or make any arrangements. Better to hide, as animals are said to do.

Several strong gusts of wind have put the highest leaves on the linden tree to flight, all together, like a flock of birds.

Farther off, in the park, leafless trees like so many candles suddenly lit by the sun when it reappeared under a curtain of black clouds. The mountaintops are not visible—but there is this little forest of burning candles at their feet, which delights.

Evening: a golden solace, like a bird landing. Like a gesture of the hand, a warmth on the forehead; or like music that slows before it falls silent, a measure to prevent any rupture.

And such a morning, birds in flight, pigeons surely, at times of a dazzling whiteness against the backdrop of golden or russet forests; a whiteness, which we might imagine would not touch us so deeply were it not a gathering-in of colours rather than a rejection or omission of them.

DECEMBER

Proust: on rereading, I was disappointed, very slightly, by his well-known description of the hawthorn; a touch too much subtlety which, with further refinement, saps some 'freshness' from what it is celebrating. On the other hand, I still find him unparalleled in worldly comedy: the evening at the Verdurins, for example, where Forcheville appears for the first time and, in sparking Swann's jealousy, immediately endows the social satire with a deeper and darker background. Applied to the human world, the refinement of Proust's analyses had depth; applied to the natural world, not always, even though his observation of the one was no less keen than his observation of the other. It is also possible that he was more talented in apprehending the impure than the pure, whatever nostalgia he always harboured for the latter.

A true winter day: that strip of relatively bright sky above the pale horizon, tenuous hills, almost transparent; and higher up, a light mass, uniformly grey, of clouds like pending snow, like a large sack of snow, set to burst at any moment.

I reread what Proust wrote about the 'little phrase', now so deservedly famous, from Vinteuil's sonata in *Swann's Way* with the kind of gratitude and joy you feel when seeing such perfect and persuasive form being given to your own essential intuitions, down to these lines that should be engraved in gold at least in memory:

> Perhaps it is not-being that is the true state, and all our dream of life is inexistent; but, if so, we feel that these phrases of music, these conceptions which exist in relation to our dream must be nothing either. We shall perish, but we have as hostages these divine captives who will follow and share our fate. And death in their company is somehow less bitter, less inglorious, perhaps even less probable.[4]

Days of fog and rain. Drops of rain hanging from the branches of the fig tree like extremely concentrated light, very pellucid small globes—more than the mistletoe seeds will be soon, for the new year—falling sometimes but only rarely; pearls, of course (and I remember the Rilke poem I recently reread about the necklace missing its clasp); musical notes, too, like those I am listening to at the same time, distinct, brilliant, of Haydn's *Piano Variations*; most surprising is their intense luminosity in the greyness that surrounds them, the density of their cold, white radiance.

'The cold season': these few pearls suspended from the fig tree's leafless branches, no longer warmed by any throat, any neck around which they would have been carefully hung.

Because of this whiteness, I suddenly think of Christian S. as we had seen him one of the last times, this summer, bringing Anne-Marie a small bouquet of wildflowers he had picked on his way, dressed all in white linen (but surely without 'candid probity'); tall and blond as he was, smiling, endowed with natural elegance, on that afternoon he seemed rather an apparition, a phantom, as if he were a messenger discreetly come from another space, a kind of Parsifal— although his had been the exact opposite of a chaste life, which may have led him to that state of despair, which his suicide revealed so brutally—because there is, after all, a kind of candour that can persist within these deviations and ultimately render them unbearable. Perhaps, as in the world of the elves, he would have had to find a tether that would have enabled him to stay in this world, those he had found for himself probably not being good ones.

Something else I should remember from Proust, in *Jean Santeuil*, which contains the seeds of several central pages of *In Search of Lost Time*.

First, on the apple orchards:

> And this infinite pleasure, through which we suddenly recognize, as we walk along an orchard, the white blossoms of the apple trees [. . .] The pleasure is a moral one [. . .] We sense that beneath the green varnish of the leaves and the white satin of the blossoms, there is some especial being, an individual we love [. . .] We have a sense [. . .] of something underneath, our pleasure seems profound . . .

Elsewhere, in 'Memories of the Sea at the Sight of Lake Geneva':

> These are beautiful hours in the life of the poet, in which chance places on his path a sensation that encompasses the past and allows his imagination to encounter the past it had not known . . .

[...]

And this profound pleasure, in justifying us for giving priority to the imagination now that we understand that it is the organ which serves the eternal, perhaps raises us as well by showing us that we feel such happiness when we are freed from the present, as if our true nature were outside of time, made to savour eternity . . .

1996

I would like never to forget those images from the documentary filmed, if I'm not mistaken, in Kazakhstan, about an eagle trainer teaching the profession to his son who was still a child. The country in which it was set was one of arid mountains, rocks, and sand; almost a desert under vast skies.

We saw the child, with a beautiful face, smooth and round, galloping and holding perched on his wrist an eagle almost as big as he was. We saw the horses, in winter, sinking up to their chests in the snow. The man's face had symmetrical features and an extraordinarily, admirably calm expression.

As with the Dalai Lama's emissary to the Kingdom of Lo: the image of a life still bound to the elementary and because of this, undeniable, great and noble. Harsh and noble like the mountains. I don't believe I mistook what I saw; these were segments of a lived epic; the last remnants, certainly the very last of what corresponds in real life to the archaic objects unearthed here and there, bits of pottery, weapons or statues. These images certified, in a sense, the beauty we find in these relics.

What, then, should we think of all that, for centuries now, has distanced us from them, in distances evermore astronomical?

Between two rain showers, a short walk along the Lez. There is decidedly something better than a rhyme between *lierre* and *pierre* ['ivy' and 'stone'], something in this dark, gnarled plant, its clinging, in both senses of the word, to very ancient things, to old walls, to ruins; to the human, which it both invades and protects and which it adorns. We find it beautiful, less as a reminder of the past than for the sense it offers of power, of stability, of duration. Green necklaces, chains or nooses.

The riverbed, considerably widened by the floods of the past few years, appears very white in this January light, as if it had carried very old bones that had become porous: an ossuary ceaselessly washed and polished by abundant, rapidly flowing water.

It's already the moment of almost imperceptible shadows on the grass because it is greener than usual at the beginning of the year—shadows as light as the gestures depicted on Attic steles which Rilke evokes in the second Duino elegy: lines that have no more weight than these shadows but as much nearly invisible power. Light has this effect sometimes. On the ground it writes the last words that still count for us.

FEBRUARY

Rereading, almost two years later, the note from February 1996: 'Teissyères: frost on the ridge,' which I was too lazy to develop. I remember it had been rather cold that day and the sky rather dark. There may have been snow on the ubacs. The path, not always clearly visible, rose towards the source of the Lez. The incline was quite steep; and all of a sudden, when we had almost reached a crest where the wind was very strong, we saw on the branches of a few trees—pines no doubt because I remember they were a very dark green—those drops of frost like so many pearls, but more brilliant than pearls, perfectly distinct, similar to glass ornaments, of course, to those glass icicles I kept in a small padded box, Christmas tree decorations from my childhood; but we cannot forget that these are drops of coldness, raindrops the cold has frozen and made to sparkle as if with a magic wand. But perhaps the sight was more amazing for being so rare, the drops glittering against a background of greenery and not of snow. A comb adorned with pearls, such as might be found on a queen's dressing table—and none of all this, in truth. But the word 'faery' would be the one if it were not so worn, so palled, so *denatured*.

The mountain, in the evening, attenuated to the point of resembling the moon when we glimpse it in the sky in broad daylight.

The sun's lamp suddenly turned on, almost blinding, beneath a bar of clouds just before sunset: six o'clock in the evening.

Must I retain anything of such 'thoughts' that came to me one night recently? These were 'questions' asked of a 'crowned poet' who was also a horse 'crowned' with scars on its knees from falls (did I mean a Pegasus after his fall?). This poet, then, was 'grabbed from behind' and led to a 'witch's mirror' which showed him the future, his death, that is, as the only certainty he could still count on. In particular, the old men showed him his house: a fir-wood coffin. The questions which returned insistently were roughly these:

'How could I have been this?'; 'How could I have been born?'; or God knows what in this line, which seemed very eloquent the night I dreamt it, or simply daydreamed about it, an eloquence that completely escapes me this morning. In any case, I told myself that I finally absolutely had to face it and stop hedging. The word 'subterfuge' emerged, only to be conclusively ruled out. I could finally think death at the risk of upsetting my supposed serenity; this task eloquently reasserted itself and contradicted the vow I had just made to write nothing but 'winged words'. The few verses that came to me in the circumstances seemed very powerful. Also present, a little off to the side, was the figure of a young girl dressed in black in whom desired grace and reviled death were no doubt united. In all likelihood, I won't draw anything from this, neither poem nor lesson. But in the obscurity of night, it did have a certain force, a certain importance for my fate; there was in it a confrontation, a battle; as well as an attempt to surpass myself.

MARCH

At the end of a dream that, as often happens, distorted, inflated mundane domestic problems, I notice four little girls crouching at the foot of a wall, all dressed in black and each carrying a small scythe—like four childlike allegories of Death. Then my companion, Yves B., with whom I was debating the aforementioned problems, explains that this is how they ritually handle the potatoes; after which I catch sight of their 'guide' bracing himself to pick up from the ground, onto which he has collapsed, a crucifix that is still attached to its stone plinth. At the sight, I entreat him to save his strength. (Evidently, I was confusing him with the friend in question, a stonemason by necessity if not by choice.)

While reading the introduction to Martin Buber's *Ecstatic Confessions* this morning, with one ear I listen to the trills of several birds in the wintery linden. I see yellowish smoke rising from the neighbour's chimney, a sign that the weather is still cold; I've also got the news of the world weighing on my mind, the fear and anxiety coming out of Jerusalem. It creates a strange sort of jumble in a tired head.

In *Ecstatic Confessions*, these words of Hildegard von Bingen (whose rediscovered musical works are very much in vogue at the moment): 'The light I see is not local; it is far, far brighter than the cloud that carries the sun. And I cannot see depth or length or breadth in it. And it is called for me that shadow of the living light.'[5]

❦

Dream. We enter, my son and I, a place that resembles a luxury hair salon to make some purchase; there, stretched out something like a canapé, was a woman whose face was not dissimilar to Monica Vitti's and whose body, veiled in transparent cloth, exhibited the perfect beauty of a Titian Venus. My son completes his purchases and is about to leave when the young woman, perfectly calm and without the slightest agitation, hints that she appreciates handsome, vigorous young men—but not at all old men, she adds (unless it was I who inferred this, not without a sense of pique, from her manner); so he stays with her and I leave, alone. I realize that I am in an unfamiliar district of a very large, modern, rather opulent city, comprised of vast spaces, expansive squares, large terraces, at one of which I am soon sitting down for a drink; and then conversing with individuals, who work with our young friend D. C. on various theatre projects, very much at ease and quite self-assured; they are true entertainment professionals, as full of self-confidence as I am lacking; they leave so that I can eat my lunch in peace. Whether or not I do, what is most essential is the more and more concentrated impression of being in an unknown city or, rather, in Paris but in outer areas I've never set foot in before. Feeling more or less lost, in any case, anxious; strolling through buildings that are evermore modern and luxurious, like the passageways of an ocean liner. At a certain point, as I continue searching for the Metro station that will get me back to familiar territory, I note that the corridor and the stairways I used have been taken over by young people whose appearances are hardly reassuring, like those you sometimes run into at the Forum des Halles; then once again I'm walking along a kind of terrace that is actually a prison courtyard, all four walls of which are occupied by young people (again!), several of whom, to my great astonishment tinged with fear, seem to be carrying rifles; and I see that one of the prisoners, this one unarmed, with a rather delicate, sickly face is leaning on the another's knees, which reminds me of the 'disciple whom Jesus loved' in representations of the Last Supper.

My search for a Metro or a bus that would allow me to escape this threatening neighbourhood drags on; but I'm now accompanied by my wife. Just when I finally discover a station sign, which I point out to her and which is called 'Leonard' (this might have come from reading, earlier that day, a text about Petrarch by the poet Zanzotto, in which he recalls a mimed charade that required him to play a lion— *leo*—then cover himself with perfume—*nard*), I once again find myself alone, my wife having lingered in a large department store, riding on a bus that continues to drive through neighbourhoods every bit as unfamiliar to me and just as vast. When I ask the driver to stop, he replies that these vehicles, Renaults, are not equipped with the kind of brakes that allow him to stop when he wishes; I therefore must resign myself to the impossibility of being joined by my companion. And yet, near the end of the dream—a dream that was never at any moment particularly sombre, either literally or figuratively—a miracle occurs: I have become a sort of visionary, able to communicate with the entire planet and renowned for this ability throughout the world; such that when I grabbed a package of biscuits, intentionally or not, from a shelf in a large department store—always vast spaces!—I was finally able to hear the voice that spoke to me through the package . . . as a result I could wake feeling reassured.

On this March afternoon, driving towards Montélimar, a great many almond trees in bloom, all the more moving for appearing as they did along a banal road under an overcast sky—like signs of friendship made to you, somewhat like the robin's cautious company; yes, always very moving, as is the first light green in the fields, while the branches of other trees, still bare, reveal shoots that are barely pink. How many more times will I see this sign? A dozen, perhaps, or with 'luck' a bit more: that isn't many. It's like a phrase that is short, inescapably short—or rather like having to cross a field and seeing the far edge distinctly—it's not the far edge itself that is distinct but the distance that separates you from it. Because the border is hidden, more or less mercifully, by the fog which is ignorance about 'the day and the hour'; and the even denser one about the 'last things'.

Once again, all around, a kind of stammering of the white flowers on the branches; which touches you even more mysteriously when they're in disorderly groups, like something dispersed, scattered, squandered. As if someone indivisible were scattering a frail coinage of more value than any other.

Bach, '*Jesu, der du meine Seele* . . . ': I think of the sea, of an ocean that, unlike the one crossed last year, would not be an endless succession of funerary mounds, a cold swell covering an even colder emptiness; but instead a movement that would carry, would lift, a supple foundation one could entrust oneself to without any fear; or an immense cradle, an enormous moving bed; or the array of muscles, feathers, and light bones in a wing.

And suddenly, over it all, over the powerful, benevolent swell, the ascending jubilation of the lark: listening to it, no grave can hold you.

APRIL

A long dream, or so it seemed to me afterwards, as not too many elements had been lost on waking.

It involved an itinerary from Jerusalem to Lausanne (at least that's what I explain at a certain moment, that I've come on foot from Jerusalem and I'm in a hurry to arrive to spare my mother, who is waiting for me, any additional worry.) I pass over an episode on my journey in which I meet a friend whose voice can hardly be heard even though it had once been rather thundering; from the scars on his neck, I surmise that he is suffering from cancer—which unfortunately is true.

More important is the fact that I am soon separated from my goal, which is Lausanne, by a very poor Arab suburb with sloping, narrow streets that resemble furrowed staircases and shacks painted a dirty white, although their inhabitants all evidence great friendliness (so much so that I write down one's address in order to send presents for his children. When someone pointed out two of them to me, infants lying on stairs and I asked how many the parents had in all, I was told a high number, maybe eight, and I allowed myself to suggest that that was quite a lot, I felt for the only occasion during my encounters in this dream, a sense of hostility that made me regret my remark).

Nevertheless, it remained essential for me to escape this excessive hospitality and finally reach my destination. I passed from this kind of kasbah to a neighbourhood with architecture that was still eastern but new and quite elegant (like the Jewish quarter rebuilt in the Old City of Jerusalem), with plenty of Arabs but they, too, appeared affluent—like the Algerian editor who had visited me a few days earlier—I thought one of them might be fundamentalist even though he was wearing European clothing. In this vast neighbourhood, beyond which I nonetheless had glimpsed Lausanne, or at least the silhouette of a city with churches that resembled it, a big celebration was being held. There were many people and roads were blocked but the crowd remained friendly and joyful. Someone to whom I'd told my story gave me a pass that allowed me to continue my journey. At the edge of a large meadow, or sports field, I was walking along, uniformed soldiers were cheerfully handling Kalashnikovs as if for a modern spectacle. So I had no other fear than the obsessive one of arriving home late. Farther on, the facade of a Catholic church, unexpected in this neighbourhood, rose up at the end of a street barred by a wall, next to said facade, that was pierced by a door such as is often found when a convent adjoins a church. Since the priest was coming towards me, I asked him if I could use the passage behind the door; at the sight of my firman, he granted me permission, but it seemed to me that he did so with less courtesy than the Arabs. On the other side of the wall, I found myself in an enormous residence that must have been a boarding house for girls; the ones I glimpsed, incidentally, were very seductive but one in particular, who started rolling around on the floors of several rooms, was frankly lascivious, a rather peculiar way of waxing the floors, I understood . . . (The words 'enormous residence' remind me that the dream had perhaps begun precisely with my crossing large rooms of old flats. I'd been struck by their run-down, untidy, and dusty appearance and by the charm of old paintings—or trumeaux; it also seems to me that in one of the sitting rooms an old gramophone was playing even though it was lopsided; it was like an animal chewing a galette bigger than its mouth . . . And it may be that an eccentric, a man still young, lived in the house.)

I woke up when, having left the 'Arab' quarter, I handed my pass, useless from this point on, to a final guard as smiling and friendly as the other residents. I'll never know, if I had remained asleep, whether or not I would finally have reached my family home and reassured my mother. (Yet I was not a child, I was the old man I am and will be from now on.)

This dream was beautiful, varied, luminous, rich and surprising from start to finish—except for the suffering figure of my sick friend, but that was like an aside or perhaps another dream. I went from one surprise to the next, still harbouring the gnawing anxiety that I would never reach my destination. But I have not managed to describe its vividness here.

Mozart, Sonata for Piano and Violin in A: I'm not surprised that the musicologist Alfred Einstein spoke of it as the soul's dialogue with God. To say things this way is to express them badly; but at the very least it designates the altitude to which this music leads you in the adagio. You could also say that if there is no God, or gods, and never were, such music would beget them; or that it seems to call, to summon them, as Hölderlin does explicitly in *The Walk in the Country*; but when done implicitly, as it is here, it's even more compelling. One could take it a step further: in this music, they have answered the call.

The church in Ethiopia during the Easter holidays: while watching this documentary, I constantly had the feeling it was fictional, a movie—in the spirit, say, of Pasolini's *Medea*. Strange, this persistence of rites well into the twentieth century, with an aspect that makes one think of Tibet in its archaism, its harshness— the landscape's arid, mountainous appearance. The beauty—there is no other word for it—of the white robes, of the sacerdotal ornaments, of a few faces, young or old; with this all the bric-a-brac of devotional images. As always, I find myself torn between fascination and rejection. The architecture itself is completely admirable and unique: rock-hewn Romanesque. (The site is that of Lalibela, dating from the twelfth century.)

That moment in early spring when light still passes through the newborn leaves before throwing a shadow (in the fig tree as it lifts all of its child hands). They turn the light into a shade of yellowish green; they catch fire like so many small candle flames in the frame, the scaffold, the monstrance of the tree. Very quickly they will become opaque, protective; for now, it's like seeing a brief smile flit over someone's face.

'They even tied up my corpse, for fear it would escape—or come back to life . . . ', words in a dream or in the state between waking and sleep. Perhaps I had thought of the Russian poets I am writing about these days.

Dream. Atop an elevation, an urban one, not rural, on a site that could resemble the esplanade of the Trocadéro, two factions or armies are preparing for battle; I'm one of the organizers. It seems to me that it was supposed to be just a game but seeing the clubs or metal bars some were arming themselves with I can only fear it would take a turn for the worst. And so I start speaking very loud, declaiming, mimicking the battle as if I were the main character, to be sure that the whole thing remain merely a spectacle—or be reduced to one.

Another moment of dream, the same night: at the end of a visit with my mother-in-law, when I was about to kiss her, her face gave way, she slowly slid to the ground and lay on her side. We were overcome with fear that this time it was the end.

Dreams again. I'm doing my military service (from which I had, in reality, been exempt at the last minute). The custom there is that conscripts are whipped on the back by one of their comrades. Here it's our children who wield the whip. Because they are my children, they go so easy on me, I fear the corporal will punish them; so I explain to him that it's perfectly natural for them to do so and he seems to accept my explanation. From then on, the entire atmosphere of the service changes to one of extreme tolerance. I notice, for example, that my son, whom I catch sight of from a distance surrounded by his comrades, is wearing a red bow tie; and my daughter, who has come to show me what she's eating in a small clay bowl, tells me that it's not bad at all.

This is followed by an episode in which she (or someone else) shows me the place where she will live from now on, a small suite of three bare, austere rooms, true cells, well isolated from the outside world; I even see myself trying to bolt with a broken latch a very small window, high up, suggesting there is some threat outside, though I do not know what.

I then found myself in a kind of small chateau, of a vaguely medieval type, with a bearded young man who resembled a number of young poets, editors or intellectuals I have met; probably Swiss. A short delivery boy arrives, not without difficulty, riding a delivery tricycle in a sloping, or rather bumpy, courtyard bringing something or other to the young resident in the chateau, who hands him some other unknown thing crudely bundled in newspapers, maybe the object of the vaguely clandestine trade off of which he would live. At this point he gave me a tour of the chateau, full of ancient objects and furniture, real or fake; I think or I'm given to understand that this may be another source of income for him. Continuing my tour alone, I push open a door and enter a rather large room in which there is, on my left, a bed; not without embarrassment, I realize that there is someone in this bed. I see the head of a young woman, neither beautiful nor ugly, who wakes but does not seem to be angry with me for my indiscretion. She rises, already dressed, and I remember only that she said to me, with regard to her companion: 'He didn't choose a cadre, strictly speaking, "of the Left" to live with,' in a tone that was more amused or resigned than critical.

Segesta: completely grey sky, rather cold wind, the ochre of the columns that are worn, decayed, as if the stone had burnt—the tall grasses, the wild flowers, the birds nesting in the cornices—and behind it, in the deep ravine with rocky, grass-covered slopes, at the very bottom, a meandering, muddy stream. As beautiful as the Valley of the Temples in Agrigento has remained with its profusion of yellow daisies and the vitality of the trees—olive, fig, almond—it is especially beautiful seen from below, when you come from Gela. Whereas here, in Segesta, you are caught up in the illusion of being in the 'truth'.

Old story. The emotion that overcomes you as nowhere else, does not deceive. It is in no way historical truth because at the time the temple was in use, it was not in ruins—that is a chestnut. Instead, it was covered with ornaments and a roof, its hearth bound by walls, and all around it was a crowd surely as colourful and boisterous as those we see in every site of pilgrimage or celebration.[7] Perhaps what is involved is a truth that was reserved for us shortly before the end of the world and well after the end of the gods for whom this temple and so many others were built— who knows? What is this truth at the end of all ends?

Maybe this one: that the centuries past have removed little by little the precarious forms that religious sentiment has donned, leaving only essential signs, all the more precious to us because we recognize clearly that they are the last, themselves doomed to disappear sooner or later; essential signs because they render perceptible the connection between the chosen site and the monument, between us and the world;

signs reduced to utmost simplicity, the steps and the worn columns getting closer to the stone that serves as their base and gradually covering itself with grasses and lichens instead of with gold. It's as if the temple's end were rejoining its beginning, its origin, the first gesture with which humans would have turned stone into stele; and as if we, the rest of us, were still capable of understanding this gesture, even of replicating it, differently, without imitating it.

Ortygia, crossed during the hour of siesta, after a delicious lunch on the sun-filled square where a wedding party was coming out of the church; the bride's train must have been several metres long; after the congratulations, the bouquets, the ballet of cars, not a living soul will remain; the narrow, shady streets will be almost empty, albeit with flowers on many of the balconies of Spanish wrought iron—my only memory of one my long-ago trips here is of these balconies; everything is decrepit and dilapidated, the churches empty or boarded up, their steps overrun with weeds; there are large wooden supports everywhere to prevent dangerously tilting facades from crumbling and mangy cats; everything is in a state of admirable abandon, dereliction—and stranger, more beautiful still are the quays lined with low houses, all asleep, if not empty as well, with very little automobile traffic and no one walking other than us; the water of sea, at our feet, is surprisingly clear. I don't know why this

waterfront, winding, humble, touches me so deeply—
vaguely reminds me of *The Desert of the Tartars* . . .

Calling the dereliction admirable, as I couldn't
help but do here and, above all, experiencing it as such
is subsequently shocking. Is it pure aestheticism? On
the contrary, I think that the emotion and the sense
nearly of exaltation experienced there, possibly due to
a small extent to the resurgence of a very distant but
intact memory—such resurgences always give your
life, your person, a feeling of continuity—arose primarily from an impression of 'truth', as in Segesta, but
in a profane register; in contrast to the sense of more
or less serious falsification given off by sites that have
been restored, whether the restoration was done well
or badly. We obviously could not delight in the fact
that this old quarter of Syracuse had become so mis-
erable and no doubt unsanitary; but it did tell the
truth, at least a truth about the passage of time, about
history: that these palaces, these churches, these
volutes, this art belongs to the past, they have been
gnawed by death and that we cannot hide or disguise
this for ever. This city somewhat resembles a grave-
yard being formed, somewhat a slow-motion ship-
wreck; although with the infinitely touching aspect
that a trace of life, of the humblest species survived in
it, as persistent as periwinkles or ivy.

The cheerful, even wonderful impression inspired
in me by the sight of the waterfront, less run-down,

less disowned than the interior, strikes me as perhaps more mysterious, more irrational. It was as if an invisible fairy had just passed, putting these low houses to sleep in broad daylight; as if, indeed—and this is what made me think of *The Desert of the Tartars*—facing the open sea as they did, they were waiting for something, what exactly was not known, as if the glittering sunlight on the sea hid more than it revealed. This impression, unlike the preceding one, seems to me to pertain only to pure reverie—albeit an ancient, still active and, at times, fertile reverie. If I could have broken into these houses, supposing a few of them were still inhabited, and then, even more impossible, into the sleep of someone who was, in fact, taking a long siesta at that hour on that day, the dreams I would have had access to would surely not have been any more-or-less magical than dreams anywhere else in the world; I would have found more or less the same mixture of the sordid and the marvellous and—who knows?—no more anxiety than in my own dreams.

Dream. Playing that childish game that consists of randomly throwing some object, a pebble, a piece of wood, ahead while out walking and being obligated to follow it, I ended up getting lost; since I am spending the holidays in the chalet that belongs to my uncle and aunt Ch., whose severity I dread, I am upset; then I am relieved at the sight of a telephone booth from which I can reassure them. (I must have forgotten the elements that made this dream interesting because what I can remember of it is not.) I spent two or three holidays in this childless couple's large chalet and these were not always my happiest times; my uncle was very fond of order and would rarely tolerate having his routines disrupted; his favourite pastime was tinkering in a workshop filled with the lovely smell of wood, something I was utterly incapable of; I already much preferred the rather well-stocked library he had inherited from his father, a professor of literature, in which I believe I'd have later found works that would have pleased me, notably Italian classics. I would gladly borrow a book and take it to the wooden pavilion at the far end of the park that surrounded the chalet—a chalet famous for having belonged to a prominent figure in Vaudois history, Louis Ruchonnet; the alpine landscape in which my 'Requiem' ends must have been inspired by the countryside visible from this refuge. I also remember the pleasure I took in listening, thanks to the gramophone in the sitting room, to Mozart's Symphony in G minor; and more vividly still, no doubt, the 'Le Chaland qui passe' sung by Lys Gauty, without having an inkling that what touched me most of all must have been the radiant femininity of her voice.

At the break of dawn, with the very first glimmers, the very first bird calls: like small embers of a fire that will take, like its first cracklings.

During the night, very close to the house, I had heard in the trees a bird call that did not resemble any I knew; a very distinct chirping, on a single note, a small cry: 'pee-ee', to which another bird answered, the reply so faint that it must have come from quite far away. The bird, no doubt too small to be visible, moved quickly, then stayed in the same tree for a long time.

Around four or five o'clock in the morning, surprised once again by the violent radiance of Venus over the mountain. A cabochon like those you can see gleaming on the crown of a Gothic king.

On Olga Sedakova, the Russian poet I was delighted to meet in Moscow. I liked what I believed I understood of that 'Epitaph', at the risk of numerous mistakes:

> In thought or in a dream, Nina, we walked
> each day along some ancient path, it seemed to
> me, following the white flagstones, fascinated.

'It wasn't the Appian, but another,' you told
me. No matter. In their cities
there were few paths
to lead you from tomb
to tomb. 'Hello!'—we heard—
'hello!' (We know the favourite word of
farewells.)
'Hello!' How clear is your gaze on beloved
ground!
I stopped: I see with the enormous world's
eyes.
Only absence looks. Only the invisible sees.
Do pick up your pace: I will pass you

Walking up from the village, once again my eyes are
drawn by the plants, the mixture of lavenders and
white, dried grass (oat or brome, I'm uncertain) whose
frail 'flowers' of graceful spurs, all turned towards the
south by the bise, make me think of the small Tibetan
prayer flags. But each of the plants on these banks, all
very common, seem to me to be mysteriously wonderful or wonderfully mysterious. Spiny restharrow,
in which the combined blue and red are so intense,
chicory and others. And I forget the end, more or less
near at this point, of the trail, which I should also envi-
sion now, with the coldest and least cowardly gaze
possible—without pathos.

Dream in which every benevolent or just amiable gesture on my part is countered with a sarcastic, rude or obscene response from various people in a room, including one or two whores. Escaping the aggression directed at me is not possible: pinching, grimacing, sarcastic remarks that amaze and frighten me; a little satanic ballet.

Dream. A visit to Moscow with very beautiful and expansive vistas, notably of buildings with golden domes on the opposite bank of a river—which would lead one to think instead of St Petersburg. From the boat we took to cross the river, I point out to Michel Rossier who is accompanying me the narrow ship with tall chimneys that recalls the beginning of the Revolution, the name of which I have trouble deciphering: *Kessel . . . ring* (it is, of course, the cruiser *Aurora*). Then we see a vague terrain with immense carnival machinery of the Ferris wheel variety and a short beggar who, dissatisfied with having received only middling alms, makes a face and limps off imitating a toad.

Serratula: like flower dust, like flowers made of pink dust; with a coarse, ragged, torn air. A mendicant colour? Then, she says: A marvellous mendicant.

AUGUST

A few notes, at first, simply to keep from forgetting. 'Flowers on the talus deprived of dew, a pitiful sight for the traveller', the opening of a Gustave Roud prose piece I once knew by heart.[8] The bindweed, white lined with pink, the one that climbs in the hedge and the other, smaller and completely pink, that blooms close to the ground, this miraculous spot of pink: What is there more beautiful? The mountain ash, the sow thistle, mallow dotting the ground, the hard earth. The hemlock.

Never have the lanes seemed more expressive; the rising path overrun with ivy. The hellebore's elegant leaves.

A single verse that survived a night spent between sleep and waking and invokes the dawn:

In bloom at last, all but eternal rose . . .

Dream. I show Anne-Marie in the contents of a magazine the title of a text by our friend Hesselbarth, who, for that matter, is not a writer but a painter; a title along the lines of: 'Impressions, Sensations and Resurrection of Lili (his wife) After her Fall.' I had decided to give this friend who had just lost his father, an Opinel knife as a gift. So there I am in an urban neighbourhood that is, to my dreamer's mind, the one in Lausanne between the Avenue Davel, on which we live, and the Place Chauderon. There is, in fact, an Opinel factory located there and I see many people entering it; a worker who comes out and approaches to tell me that if I want, as seems to be the case, to buy a knife, I have chosen a bad day because it's the official visiting day at the factory for the 'Opinels' (or 'Opinelians')—that must indicate some sort of organization of 'Friends of Opinel'; however, a bit farther up the road there is a small merchant by the name of Carmoni who sells them.

So I set out in search of this stall. The setting has changed; because of the name, perhaps, and I wonder whether it should be pronounced Carmóni or Cármoni; the surroundings resemble a neighbourhood in a small Italian city built on a rather steep slope. When I ask where I could find the said Carmoni, a little old man starts telling me; another, who has approached, corrects his instructions so that my search becomes, like the area itself, more and more confused. I remember passing on my way up the slope a tree with unusually shaped flowers or falling seeds; someone tells me that they will embed themselves in the ground at a certain moment—a bit like torches—and immediately sprout into as many small new trees. Farther on, I notice a kind of small church spire planted in the soil that resembles the tip of a Christmas tree made of red-painted plaster. As a matter of fact, there is a church facade in the vicinity. I keep asking for Carmoni's stall (firmly accenting the second syllable). '*Busco Carmoni*' —mixing up, as I sometimes do, Italian and Spanish— upon which a very thin old woman answers, '*Lo tro-vereto quà*'; that is, in a grotto dug at the foot of a cliff, which I approach, still climbing the slope. I wake. It's around seven in the morning: a very transparent and frigid dawn; the paving stones on the terrace are damp. I believe I can still make out Sirius to the east, high in the clear sky.

SEPTEMBER

Grass seen against the light, still sprouting, rather sparse, slender and straight: almost a filter, a harp . . . or, close to the ground, my last lyre. To make the evening light, which is almost golden, resound in the gusts of the already frigid wind.

On my wrist, the little butterfly with orange-brown wings that are yellow underneath: a miniscule, double stained-glass window in an utterly modern style. It spends a long time palpating my skin. A delicate, mobile stained-glass window for the sun that has finally returned.

Late at night: the crescent of the waning moon, Orion already high to herald the cold, to recall the old hunter who never ceases aiming at us, Venus with a name more tender than her radiance, Sirius twinkling—discharges from automated 'rifles' to disperse the game for the imminent opening of the other hunt—and the dreams, their often insignificant oddity; astonishment at what we have 'in our heads' and at what there is under the vault of the night sky. Order and disorder.

Rereading *Reveries of a Solitary Walker* to verify whether or not I was correct in seeing this book as a distant source and model of my own: I find that Rousseau, aside from the fifth and justly famous reverie in which he describes the ecstasy he experienced in a moment of harmony with the cosmos, says relatively little about nature and much more about psychology, morality or—hardly surprising—himself. Then, rereading *The Green Notebook*, I see that Maurice de Guérin is much more precise in his descriptions, as if his gaze, less narcissistic, were sharper and more attentive. I am surprised and as taken by these pages as I was when I first discovered them in 1943; perhaps even more than I was then.

In the final pages, written when he was twenty-four—he would die five years later—this voice that was merely poignant, becomes firmer, expands. Just as Roud, a century later, will write his first book, *Adieu*, to lament having lost the power of speech and thus, in fact, to ward off that loss. Maurice de Guérin finds his voice in the very moment he fears the drying up of his inspiration:

> It will soon be eight days since my inner life began to wane, since the river ebbed in such a noticeable reduction that, after a few rounds of the sun, it was nothing more than a trickle of water. Today I watched the last drop flow past.

Music is born from the sense of the end:

> Today I am casting only shadows, all forms are opaque and tinged with death. As in a nocturnal stroll, I advance with the isolated

sense of my existence surrounded by the inert
phantoms of all things.

We begin to hear a tread at once solemn and secret,
at the very limits of silence, the outermost reaches; a
harmony extremely close to that of Hölderlin's
Hyperion, of Novalis' *Hymns to the Night*, not only a
harmony: an experience, a thought drawn from life—
even this meagre life—an orientation of existence
towards the search for the most profound hearth:
'Nature has admitted me to the most remote of its
divine dwellings.' (It's striking that Ramuz, who
intended to devote a thesis to Guérin had begun by
imitating him; and that, one generation later, the
young Chappaz had similarly been pervaded by him.
The sentiment of having no more existence than a
shadow is not all that Roud laments anew in certain
of his most beautiful prose passages: 'Such is the
nature of my thoughts: a wisp of hovering vapour.')

I return to the end of *The Green Notebook*: not
long after 2 February 1835, the date of the death of
Marie de la Morvonnais, the wife of Guérin's young
friend Hippolyte, whom he mentions for the first time;
this shade, like Sophie for Novalis, becomes his guide:
'She has vanished from the visible world; she belongs
to the realms of thought . . . ' A most delicate music
accompanies this adieu, *is* this adieu. 'I've abandoned
the idea of her earthly existence. I have erased it from

the external world . . . '; 'I go on, I imagine as best I can the dwellings of pure spirit . . . '; 'The weightless, silent footsteps of my imagination return once again to the beloved paths . . . ' There is here a constant osmosis between interior and exterior that is particularly natural to him: the murmuring of thought, the murmuring of trees.

> They [his thoughts] await life, the future, the advent of existence's successive mysteries by fortifying each other with the eloquence of intimate exhortations or they remain silent at intervals to listen to the bubbling of philosophy's secret torrent that runs beneath several existences like those streams that flow through cloisters . . . '

(What was he thinking of here? As for me, I seem to remember being surprised at the sight of a channel of water running through the kitchen of the Alcobaça monastery in Portugal. But had I not seen it, I still would have been brought up short by these words which unite what is most rapid and spirited with the immobile and silent contemplation intrinsic to monasteries in the movement of a sentence that grazes the essential.)

October 13, the last entry in *The Green Notebook* already rings of the prose in *The Centaur*: 'I travelled.

I no longer remember what movement of my fate carried me from the banks of a river to the sea . . . '

(Already we think of Rimbaud's more adventurous, violent soul: 'I had to travel, to distract the enchantments gathered in my mind. On the sea that I loved as if it could wash me clean of stain . . . ')

(Guérin or the supreme art of playing. But as a Couperin much less in accord with himself and with his century.)

The passage I just quoted ends with these words: 'Oh, who will expose me on this Nile? . . . ' He was, no doubt, thinking of Moses' basket, rescued by a tender-hearted Egyptian woman, which evokes and creates another connection, this one to Poussin.

While I still had a reasonably clear memory of *The Centaur*, which Rilke translated, I had completely forgotten the *Pages sans titre* [Untitled Pages], written shortly after he had finished *The Green Notebook* and young Marie's death; they filled me with astonishment. Almost one hundred years before Rilke identified in the last Duino Elegy with a young man following in the footsteps of the Laments towards the fountainhead of joy through an increasingly arid and silent landscape, Guérin had followed a deceased young woman on 'dark and silent paths' that lead to a metamorphosis of an adieu into abundance so long as the being is, so long as we are, confidently open to the world. Guérin had only just expressed this opening when in rushed, as if through a hole in a dike, the chorus of Muses, that is to say, myth, the Greek mythology that he revived almost as powerfully, as limpidly as Hölderlin not long before him; that is also to say, the cosmos, its slow, harmonious motion commanding his thought and his prose as he creates the constellations.

But Maurice de Guérin's specific trait, no doubt because he was destined to die young and had a premonition of this ('My soul is placed under a dying day . . . '), is that he writes 'in the glow of decline', preferring autumn over any other season, and evening over any other time of day; from then on, he will express better than anyone else the decrescendo, the rallentando of all endings, yet arriving at a silence that is no more the void than the one that succeeds a piece of music, arriving at an end that is not a conclusion or a wall; because, moreover, he accepts the slope that becomes confused with what he admirably calls Marie's 'pure, inclined confidence':

> Well, my friend, my spirit has not ceased walking in her pure, inclined confidence or rapidly descending the slope of its icy mountain towards the valleys teeming with life . . . [. . .] Similar to the prairie stream that flows over a bed of bent grass, my soul will follow its slope in nature with a soft bubbling . . .

In this, too, he prefigures Rilke who so loved the words '*Neige*' and '*Neigung*', equivalent to the word 'penchant' which so intimately binds the senses of 'leaning' and tender 'inclination'.

As for *The Centaur* that opens with the image of a cave, that mixes the times and the rivers, and that also ends with an admirably serene decrescendo, what is there to say of it other than that it is, with its fusion of nature and myth in music, here verbal, there pictorial, a large painting by Poussin, only veiled by more melancholy, being two centuries older?

Just once more, let him be heard speaking of constellations in *The Bacchante*:

> I wanted a walk along the mountains' escarpments to engender in me a mood similar to the one the stars draw from their courses, my path bringing me to the tops of the mountains as they rise through the degrees of the night sky.

NOVEMBER

The elongated leaves of irises; seen from above, like large starfish abandoned by summer on a sandy shore. Beyond them, yellow bundles of vines. And towards the sun now set—it will soon be six o'clock in the evening—that green of a field, which is the same one that intrigued me a long time ago and which appeared in certain texts, namely, in *Le Travail du poète* [The Poet's Work] and somewhere in *Obscurity*; that dark, almost maternal green, that seems to hide— or nourish—individuals, to shelter them, to rescue them so they can return, silently, tenderly, to us.

As I write, everything has grown even darker, but not without a few moments when the admirable shade of yellow flares or continues to smoulder or without the ochre of the foliage, through which glimmer the headlights' vivid stars.

The book by Takemoto, in which he recalls Malraux's encounter with Japan, even if Takemoto's fervour for the writer renders his terms at times excessive, centres on an experience that is important to me, that of 'places of convergence'. Did Malraux really experience an 'illumination' at the Nachi Waterfall? It's not certain; but there is little doubt that it was an important encounter for him; and that it is similar to my more modest ones in less illustrious, less sacred places is clear. And it could be that this unexpected convergence explains the admiration I've always had for this *oeuvre* that is so far removed from my own experience.

Takemoto quotes the statements made by the painter Kama in *Man's Fate*, who is modelled on the Japanese artist Kondō Kōichiro:

> For me, it's the world that counts [. . .] The world is like the characters of our writing [. . .] Everything is a symbol. To go from the symbol to the thing symbolized is to deepen your understanding of the world, to move towards God . . . [. . .] We can communicate even with death . . . That's what is most difficult, but perhaps it is the meaning of life.

Takemoto believes that in Japan, Malraux had encountered what he calls the '*encompassing*', which is also, apparently paradoxically, an open space in which man and the world would no longer be in confrontation. Such a space greatly resembles Rilke's '*Weltinnenraum*' [absolute inwardness of the world], his 'Open'; in which Malraux would have found the resolution of the confrontation with destiny that is central to his *oeuvre*, moving beyond the notion of heroes. We certainly cannot deny that the geniuses closest to his heart have been Rembrandt, Goya, Beethoven, even Hugo, geniuses at battling the night, at combating death like some of his fictional characters. Takemoto imagines no less than that at the end of his life, Malraux had glimpsed the serenity as expressed and developed in Japanese music.

Takemoto also quotes a passage on poetry without giving a source which seems to refer to the poetry in works of art: '[W]hat we call poetry is perhaps the presence, suddenly made discernible, of a harmony with the universe.'

I would gladly make that phrase my own. But adding, once again, this question: Is this experience of 'harmony' pure illusion or not? Taking account of the fact then that everything art has produced of the highest beauty and greatest magnificence is the product of an illusion—which flies in the face of common sense . . .

The thoughts of Proust since *Jean Santeuil*, that is, before their definitive version, belong to the same order of ideas, first on an apple orchard: 'We sense [. . .] that there is something underneath, our pleasure seems profound . . . '; and later, when Lake Geneva reminds him of the sea, a first draft of the fundamental experiences in *In Search of Lost Time*, on the imagination as 'the organ which serves the eternal' for us who 'feel such happiness when we are freed from the present, as if our true nature were outside of time, made to savour eternity . . . '

Elsewhere, when Proust recalls a winter storm in Brittany and the wind that wakes poetic inspiration, for him, that is, the production of *full ideas*—not empty ones, like those that relate only to ourselves and imitate reality without transcending it; for example, imagining amorous conquests, social successes—ideas that are 'more real' because they link the present with the past:

> Indeed, he found that he was no longer devouring life with a sense of anxiety at seeing it disappear under pleasure, instead he was tasting it with confidence, knowing that one day or another he would find again the reality contained in these minutes—as long as he did not actively seek it—in the sharp reminder of a gust of wind, in the smell of a woodfire, in the sight of a dull sky, sunlit but with a threat of rain, hanging low over the roofs.

Ideas that are full because they take in the 'essence' of our lives, the essence of our relations with the world; full ideas as opposed to empty ideas, a relation not unlike Musil's opposition of 'dead ideas' to 'living ideas'.

Thus it is that great novelists, very different from each other, meet in profound comprehension of what basically is poetry, which also brings together their works in their moments of highest achievement.

Assembling such works is to resist nihilism, especially today's bastardized forms of it. Their proliferation can disgust; or just as well, in reaction, energize.

To return to Takemoto's views, specifically, his view in *L'intemporel* [The Timeless], not about the waterfall of Nachi itself but about the famous work that portrays it, like other masterpieces of Japanese art: 'We sense that the painter neither represents nor interprets a spectacle. He hopes to have received the confidence of the world'—and of a world, unlike ours, 'free from struggle and without sin'. For art of the Far East 'appearance leads to the absolute' and 'the world *is* convergence.'

In the same work, gazing at statues at whose feet people gather to pray, Malraux writes that they belong not to an art of expression, but an art of '*accession*'. More than once, without thinking too much about it, I had the intuitive sense that every great book, especially of poetry, allowed us to *access* a world, opened us up to the world: nothing more, nothing less.

Nuno Júdice. May I for a long time to come still be able to love and make others love poems like his, like this one:

Leave: as if you had to be forgotten,
leaving behind the shadow of an image.
    Do not
take with you the words we exchanged,
like letters, at the moment of farewell; but
don't forget the evening light
sheltered in your eyes. Now and again I will
    remember
you. As if, when I turn back, you will still
be waiting, without a smile, to tell me
that time resolves everything. I do not listen
    to you; and
as I near your arms, I see you
disappear. Later, I think, this will be
part of a poem; but you insist. Love
calls us from life's interior; it requires us
to renounce the soul's immobility, to sacrifice
the body to remembered desire.

Rain and fog: light a lamp in their midst, like a piece
of fruit in straw.

In Paul Claudel's commentary on the Song of Songs,
we sometimes recognize the great poet beneath the
dogmatism; as when he hears the song of a turtle dove:

What melancholy! In the solemn accomplishment of all the year's promises, this is the part made to the irremediable, the inconsolable . . . It's the immeasurable reproach underlying all accomplishments, the grim warning of something else . . .

Opening, always opening—or for as long as possible. What opens to the light of the sky: the flower low to the ground. Like some obscurity that would blossom along with the break of dawn. The morning glory: so many tidings of dawn scattered at our feet.

Reading *Les Misérables*, truly a great book; but how naive are the hopes that inspire Hugo with the idea of Progress with a very large capital P! What would he think today? Even then the optimist counted above all on compulsory education (like Michel Serres today). As if the SS hadn't gone to school, even to catechism class!

In Claudel's commentary on the Song of Songs mentioned above, rich in surprising, substantial insights, we read in a passage on the grove of nut trees, a description of a nut, which Ponge would not have blushed to have written; it is followed—such are the rules of the game—by an interpretation: 'And so in this kind of nourishing stone, which does not dispense with an effort so that we may enjoy it, slowly developed within obscure and bitter circumstances, there is nothing that will prevent me from seeing the symbol of dogmatic truths', etc. Yet aren't nut groves like those one passes on the narrow roads of Isère actually much more mysterious, more elusive than that? When carefully weighed, aren't both his description 'à la Ponge', materialist if you will, and the allegorical—or philosophical—interpretation too simple, don't they miss the essential? That is no doubt what I will conclude after rereading the Song of Songs as recreated by St John of the Cross if I were to finish it. Something in the remarkable web of words goes beyond all interpretation with an almost childish freedom.

Violent wind churning the last remaining leaves, which are exactly similar to flocks of birds in the way they abandon the trees; and the first snowflakes fallen from the high clouds are carried away to the south; without the sun being completely veiled.

1997

JANUARY

'*Singing the earth's glory in order to no longer see it,*'
could this line from 'Requiem' regain meaning for me
now? But I would no longer talk of 'singing the glory'
of anything or anyone whatsoever; I would just greet
in passing and, with my greeting thank, what borders
a road reaching its end without wanting to think about
it too much: half out of apprehension, half out of wisdom, perhaps.

The pink bindweed flowers, observed, greeted
before I am no longer able to, before being confined
with the more or less aggressive, more or less offen-
sive devils of the final degradation.

There is no horror in the withering of flowers;
does the horror come with the 'soul'?

Hugo, in his admirable poem 'Dante's Vision' evokes the procession of kings:

> Before each phantom in the icy mist,
> Vaguely resembling an overturned cross,
> Came a bare broadsword, straight, steady
>   in the wind,
> Held by no hand and seemingly alive.

This procession in an indistinct space reminded me of one of the most powerful passages in *Les Misérables*, the one in which, just before dawn on the outskirts of Paris, Jean Valjean and Cosette watch a chain gang of convicts pass. Hugo is at his greatest when he looks into the unclear, into the mist, twilight, or darkness. The boundless exalts him. He often goes astray in it.

In the same splendid poem, a bit before, are verses that foreshadow Péguy:

> For you are the hope of those driven away
> For you are a homeland to the exiled,
> For you are port, asylum and domicile . . .

Something in Nuno Júdice makes me think of Borges when he attempts to resuscitate deceased characters from the past, like the canon Amador

Gomes in *Practice*, a tenderness filled with melancholy for all that is absent, reduced to a simple, spare inscription. The voice circulates between the people and the objects like a breath of air. As in the admirable 'Elegy', which is another attempt to collect water that is leaking away, to heal the wound of disappearance. Shades, phantoms, black figures—and the season of autumn; empty houses, abandoned gardens: always the mysterious metamorphosis of loss.

> . . . Why not return to the light of day,
> to the company of birds waiting
> for the first ships raising their nets?
>
> Because there is no one on the other side . . .

As if echoing a letter from a young poet friend raising yet again his scruples about any celebration of natural landscapes today, I read in Théodore Agrippa d'Aubigné's *Misères* [Woes]:

> . . . yet the waves of a clarity
> once rivalling pearls and sapphires
> are reddened with our dead; the soft sound
>   of their flows,
> their pleasant murmur knocks against the
>   bones.

D'Aubigné denouncing the mores of Henri III's court in the harshest terms: we forget that such excesses are nothing new when judging our own times.

Schubert's Piano Sonata in B-flat Major played by Clara Haskil: the work I always return to, but how to speak of it? What is it, especially in the first movement, that brings me nearly to tears? I cannot come up with anything better than this, once more, the sense of traversing a limit, a wall, of moving within the 'Open', the space that is both internal and external which Rilke imagined for his angels to move about in and which is the very one to which, according to Musil, the 'other state' gives you access. But it's necessary to try to explain that movement within this sphere is not at all abstract or disembodied; it has grain, colour, impulses and slumps—it is not pure jubilation; in it, lament, nostalgia, even desire are transfigured with an apparent naturalness in accordance with what could be the breath of intimate being; sorrow or anguish do not imprison in this space, instead, in some sense, they blossom.

Schubert again, the lieder sung by Elisabeth Schumann: for me listening to this is connected to an entire world of images that can only be situated in Germany, even if—is it really necessary to specify?—the vocal work I am thinking of here never has any touch of 'regionalism' about it: the paintings of Caspar David Friedrich with the figures seen from behind, lost in the contemplation of space, of city silhouettes with bell towers, of bastions—the reason the view of Estavayer in the summer haze on the other side of Lake Neuchâtel always reminded me irresistibly of Hölderlin—roads with horses, young blonde girls—many dirt paths or roads, a hilly countryside with the glow of the snow-covered Alps in the distance (as in my native country); a vagabond atmosphere (the journeys of Wilhelm Meister, of Anton Reiser), great elation and profound melancholy (and almost the same roads still travelled by a man like Roud)—human life and work still connected to the ancient world: millers, shepherds, fishermen—'*Gemütlichkeit*', the Biedermeier style: this sense of intimate comfort, without splendour or great imagination—compared to Romanticism in the manner of Hugo, notably, to all his Gothicizing or Orientalizing extravagances . . . Yes, Roud's house in Carrouge and his life were essentially still very close to that world.

> *Du lachst wohl über den Träumer,*
> *Der Blumen im Winter sah*

(You may laugh at the dreamer / Who saw flowers in winter), Roud saw the flowers, as Schubert evokes them in one of the most beautiful songs in *Winterreise*, on his windows every winter—and the drawing of the melody over these two verses could melt even the iciest interior.

MARCH

The first bloom, the first blossoms of early spring, almost painful this year because their expression only reaches me from a distance (let's put it this way); perhaps also because I can't chase away the fear that I won't see many more; which casts on them a shadow similar to the shadow of one of those clouds that, in this season, can still cross a calmer sky.

Editing the notes from my trip to Israel leads me to reread Celan's last poems and the commentary on them ventured by his Jewish friend whom he'd found again so belatedly in Jerusalem. As on each rereading, this approach oppresses me—making it more difficult to continue this work. Which words, measured against these words, would not appear too vague, too light, almost vain?

Despite it all, the garden: violets, both purple and white; flowering trees surrounded by nascent greenery, etc. Well! Despite it all, I must continue speaking. There is in Celan's intransigence, in his genius, a haughty, abrupt power that impresses me but it's not the only way. The error, the absurdity would simply be to believe one has the right to ascend all these steep summits—from which, by the way, he never spoke as a master, as I have reproached Char of doing.

Celan again:

truth,
you need
every stalk.

The light at the close of day, before dusk, in this early March resembles a wing beating in the trees, a dove. The trunks, the still-bare branches reverberate and enroot the light. While the ephemeral murmurs, seems to speak to me in veiled terms, in white and pink. The speech of the insignificant, of froth. The day we tell ourselves: You'll no longer hear such speech very often, even in the best case. And so, the point sharpens, rends and heals, irremediable. You must listen all the more closely, tune your ears to hear through the cries of hatred, the cracking of whips.

Dream from last night, half lost by my terrible memory. It was about Musil, whom I had to retranslate with his help and in his presence: so many pages to rework with the apprehension of not being able to get to the end and one page in particular, previously unpublished, the title of which was more or less: 'The Romans Do Not Do More', a phrase immediately transposed into an image of people lined up behind I no longer remember what—a wall, a barrier?—such that only their heads were visible as in certain paintings from the late nineteenth century, Degas or Vallotton, depicting loges; the heads or, rather, the hats, even mostly just the top of the hats, battered fedoras—so that one immediately concludes that the people there are poor, are beggars; hence the title, which could signify—I wouldn't swear to it since the memory is so vague—that the Romans had given them only meagre alms.

A stroll at the Roche de l'Oie, above Pierrelongue. In the pine trees. Many of the orchards have already lost their flowers, others are in full bloom. The most beautiful are like foam badly hung on the slopes. The grass is thicker in the olive groves and I remember Mallorca where this first moved me as it did in Greece later; a vague idea of a cradle, of tender sleep under these silvery cinders, around these ageless trunks, twisted like old flames that have gone cold, gnarled columns for a shepherds' walkway.

D'Aubigné, in a commentary on a psalm written after the death of his wife: 'I am no longer one of those to whom greenery brings some hope . . . '

The almost-yellow foliage of the poplars, almost orange on some; and the young pine cones, they too are almost orange. The very first oak leaves in pale shoots on trees covered with grey or silver lichen, chipped trees, half-sere and hollow—too easy an image of our old bodies and their final 'productions' or blossoming.

While listening again to Mozart's *Requiem*, if I'm not mistaken, I noted down the idea—I no longer remember why—of a 'line' passing rapidly over everything, as the white bird, the egret flew over the lake at Saint-Blaise once; but this time I imagined it in the sky over Jordan.

An arrow? A rapid sound, soaring, which did not prevent it from being something very real, very firm, fleeting and real: like a signature? a flourish? A line of iron, of lightning—but which, far from being destructive, would have signed a kind of clear promise.

I am taking up St John of the Cross' *Spiritual Canticle* again. There is much to be drawn from Valente's *La Piedra y el centro* [The Stone and the Centre]:

> Such is the strange adventure of poetic expression, the adventure of beginning perpetually begun: the adventure of dawn. The knight Don Quixote sets out at dawn. 'It must have been dawn'; but Alonso Quixano had kept vigil over his armour all night. And St John of the Cross writes: 'It [verse XV] says that this tranquil night is not like the dark night, but like night when it nears the waking of dawn.'

APRIL

In *The End of Satan*, Victor Hugo did not hesitate to take up the Song of Songs, which under his pen became 'The Song of Bethpage', a beautiful poem:

> Our songs, scattered on the breeze,
> Cross in the air
> Like arrows of opposing armies

We also find the two admirable lines about the woman: 'She keeps her feet close like those of angels.' And: 'The form of her shadow gladdens the fields.'

Dream fragments: In a corner of the terrace grapevine trellis, exactly as is in real life, I see a large bird perched, which proves to be a young duck. He lands or falls on the ground; I find him completely plucked and curled up just like those you buy ready to cook. But I see that he's moving very slowly, that he's stretching out, and is therefore alive; he's even moving his head. I'm more delighted than surprised; and I hurry off to find a pot saucer to give him water to drink and revive him; but I take a somewhat maniacally long time to wash off the little bit of dirt on the saucer; and strangely, I am irritated by this slowness which, after all, is entirely my own doing. My memory of the dream ends there.

In another, I see high above me, very far away, almost at the very top of a red building, on a kind of landing from which an outside staircase descends to the street, a woman fighting off a man's assault. Having managed to escape him, she rushes down the stairs, but the man chases her. I find her at the base, shut up in a kind of barred cage, like those for big cats in the circus, where she is safe from the tamer who is still threatening her. The man is very ordinary, a kind of Claude François, but not as soft or coquettish.

In the garden this morning, all the lanterns of the irises were lit in light blue, blue lamps in the blue light. Lanterns of water.

I just read *The Black Bird in the Rising Sun*, one of the few books by Claudel that I did not know yet. How can he be accused of not being open to the Far East when, forgetting his dogmatism, he spoke of it with such admiration? Of Noh, for example, which is not, after all, an easily accessible art form (I remember what we were able to see at the Carrière de Boulbon a few years ago, so extraordinarily beautiful at times and so abstruse).

Thus Claudel on the *shite*:

> With a movement of his magic fan, he swept the present away like vapour and with the slow wind of this mysterious wing he ordered what no longer existed to emerge around him. With the conjuration of a phrase that fades as another follows, the garden under the world gradually took shape in the sonorous ashes . . .

'*Somnambulic drama*': How well that captures at least the impression one has of it!

Later in the book: 'It seems that each movement must overcome death, with the weight and border of the immense garment, and is a slow copy of a defunct passion.' Everything he says in this regard about the sleeve and, above all, about the fan: 'On this statue, it is the only thing that trembles . . . '

That the gaze, in the East, is turned upwards. The eye rises 'like a bird, descends on the rain's path'. 'He who looks up from below awaits and prays, he who looks straight ahead desires and conquers, he who looks down from above dominates and possesses . . . '

Just as there exists a discreet if not secrete fraternity—less and less discreet, by the way—of spirits who are moved by Morandi's painting as if by a language become very rare, a language at the same time intimate and not at all subjective, there exists a family of spirits who have been fascinated for a long time by portraits from Fayum; moreover, the members of one and the other are often the same and this is not at all surprising. (Besides, when leafing through the book Jean-Christophe Bailly devoted to these portraits, *L'apostrophe muette* [The Silent Apostrophe], I was stunned by the plate with the colour reproduction of the *Man Holding an Olive Branch* to see at what point this branch, pink-and-green against the white of his robe was close to the palette and maybe even to the touch of the great painter from Bologna.)

Bailly has written very pertinent pages about the portraits; yet that still wouldn't be much of an accomplishment if his language, through a kind of muted vibration and lightness in gravity, were not so very worthy of his subject; because these portraits look at us from 'the threshold of the land of the dead', from a place about which one should not speak in a louder voice than they themselves do. In contrasting the Egyptians' beliefs about death to the Greeks' without wanting to invalidate one with the other, Bailly touches on the essential.

> For the terrifying silence of the Styx, the 'land that loves silence' substitutes another silence which includes death in the full account of the living, which associates life and death in the tension of a communal hearing. The Styx, which for the Greeks is at once a current and a hole and which, according to Hesiod, the gods themselves 'loathe', is like a death within death, like a continuously active memory of chaos. As such it is close to the Egyptian

non-world, the threat of which is always suspended. But while the Styx seems contiguous
to Hades and the latter remains a vague
dwelling and appears pervaded with darkness, the Egyptian response to the threat of
chaos finds in death itself the clarity of an
escape. For Cerberus' fury, it substitutes a
silent dog: a god who knows.

Later in the book:

> What these portraits show us is all the vio-
> lence of that which throws life into life, but as
> if gently gathered on the border where life
> disappears [. . .] The gaze symbolizes noth-
> ing, recounts nothing, it is silent, it is unfath-
> omable, mute in a way that even a silent
> mouth is not, it has before it the world it
> entered and from which it is about to depart:
> the gaze does not say farewell, it is the
> farewell . . .

For the first time, while reading this book, I thought
of how much Rilke would have liked these works (but
I don't recall that he ever mentioned them), Rilke
who, with bearing of a modern, without any more
support than a nostalgia for the sacred, haunted these
shores, this boundary between life and death, and

dreamt with such intensity that it vanished, that it was erased for Orpheus, that it is still vanishing for the angels he had invented.

JUNE

In my summer reading, Bailly again, whose *Le Propre du language* [The Particularity of Language], which I am reading with the same sense of connivance with which I read *The Silent Apostrophe*, intensified by the fact that it occasionally addresses the world's minuscule realities which I firmly believe have been speaking to me with ever-greater tender insistence as time passes; a connivance almost mingled with resentment when I admit to myself more than once that I would not have been able offer as good an account.

On flowers: '[T]his blossoming that seems to be an offering is in fact sovereign and is not addressed to anything, the flowers neither pray nor sing, the rose belongs to no one' (Angelus Silesius' words). This is exactly the same intuition I had, not right away but over time, and around which I am not done circling.

As for fireflies, whose strange enchantment I had discovered not long before, what is there to say of them after this:

These miniscule creatures, blinking as their wings beat against their luminescent bodies, seem to be prowling but like souls free of suffering, like words not yet pronounced. Souls of nothing, without precedence, living only for a nocturnal, nuptial celebration . . .

How can one be so precise without killing the mystery, in fact, even deepening it if possible? Pages that extend reflections on tombs:

In Salzburg, in St Peter's Cemetery under the rockface, or in the Greek islands, a candle burns on every tomb. In the oil lamp's weak light lives a soul that dissolves in memory. Although anonymous, the burning lamp nonetheless has more power than the name and escapes. Representing the deceased or the thought one has of him, the lamp, in its tenuousness, resides in that space and answers to the night sky: it would be sweet to imagine the earth like such a celestial design, the lamps of the dead silently answering the stars. Here, like a moth glued against a windowpane, lands the idea of a World reduced to this habitation, to these vestiges and, oddly, instead of inspiring fear, this vision of a sleeping world illuminates for an instant: 'eternal rest' surrounded by various kinds of fireflies.

And this, too, on mystery:

> Mystery is ineffable because it neither can nor
> should be described. Around it, only rumour
> spreads—a 'they say' that says nothing, that
> remains silent, that says one must not speak.
> But as a result, it is all of language, every pos-
> sibility of phrasing, that is nailed to this
> silence: not so much limited by it as incurring
> the prestige, roaming around the initiation as
> in a blind dance haunted by a gleam of light.
> And most mysterious of all, actually, is that
> this gleam could subsist, that the memory of
> the gods or what they named could persist in
> remaining silent within the language that had
> become separated from them . . .

Not long ago, I almost met Bailly in the rooms of the
Magnani-Rocca Foundation outside of Parma, which
has some magnificent Morandis, around which he had
just organized a small event that was meant to be
staged shortly after my visit yet about which I was not
aware. No matter. I've been crossing paths with him
often for some time now wherever this gleam sur-
vives, a gleam that in my eyes is more important than
anything else and that stubbornly remains just steps
away from silence, there where Anubis' black dog
rests his paw on us, at once menace and assistance.

Yunus Emre, translated by Yves Régnier (formerly in the Metamorphoses series):

> I weep. It is my destiny. Weep from now on, my eye. My tears flow like a stream of blood. Murmur from now on, my eye.
>
> God has thrown me into these flames. I am consuming myself. It is my destiny. Do not laugh again, my eye, for the rest of my life.
>
> Disregard the future. Disregard this dying rose. Disregard this whitening night. Disregard from now on, my eye.
>
> Do not let yourself be fooled by apparent beauty. Do not taste the poisoned honey. Do not believe the illusory, my eye, and do not dream any more from now on.
>
> Yunus Emre, what is the matter? Your words express the evident. We are walking towards the horizon of seas. Do not retreat from now on, my eye.

JULY

I must recall some fragments of Thoreau's *Walden*, too, some of those one would happily collect with so many others gathered over the course of a life of reading into a kind of 'survival kit':

We must learn to reawaken and keep ourselves awake, not by mechanical aids but by an infinite expectation of the dawn, which does not forsake us in our soundest sleep. [. . .] To affect the quality of the day, that is the highest of arts . . . [9]

[. . .]

Time is but the stream I go a-fishing in. I drink at it; but while I drink, I see the sandy bottom and detect how shallow it is. Its thin current slides away, but eternity remains. I would drink deeper; fish in the sky, whose bottom is pebbly with stars. I cannot count one . . .

[. . .]

The grass flames up on the hillsides like a spring fire,—"et primitus oritur herba imbribus primoribus evocata"—as if the earth sent forth an inward heat to greet the returning sun; not yellow but green is the color of its flame—the symbol of perpetual youth, the grass-blade, like a long green ribbon, streams [. . .] It grows as steadily as the rill oozes out of the ground. It is almost identical with that, for in the growing days of June, when the rills are dry, the grass blades are their channels, and from year to year, the herds drink at this perennial green stream, and the mower draws from it betimes their winter supply. So our human life but dies down to its root, and still puts forth its green blade to eternity.

AUGUST

David Mus' very free transposition of Shelley's 'Ode to the West Wind' which he would not have done without the example of André du Bouchet, revealed the ode to me as truly a great gust of wind from off-shore (badly versed in English poetry as I am, I had never read Shelley's poem). On those sultry days, I received the mists full in the face like a cool benediction along with the poem's closing certitude revived in French by Mus:

> *Ô Ouest,*
> *cher vent,*
> *l'hiver arrive;*
> > *sur ses pas quelques part*
> > *doit marcher l'Avril.*

[Oh West, / dear wind, / winter is coming; / April must be following / somewhere not far behind.][10]

❧

These very few words follow that reading note:

> '*La corbeille de fruits—l'enfant*'
> [The basket of fruit—the child]

I imagine, reading them again after several months, that the internal rhyme that led me to bring them together was the plumpness, the freshness, the fullness of the one and the other; and something still less simple, less clear, because I would not have forgotten for a single instant what distinguishes a human being from an apple, even if both had round cheeks with a fresh colour: the look, the smile, the first words, because of these there is something invisible in a face that is capable of sight.

The bindweed, seen again this morning on the hillside of the Bertrands' house: what shouldn't be touched with words and, at the same time, what matters to me perhaps most of all in the act of putting into words. 'The pure of source is a riddle', wrote Hölderlin in *The Rhine*: this is what I return to persistently, hesitating yet again as if at a crossroads in which one road leads to a long, humble and patient search and the other requires a swift apprehension that could only be translated into words with grace.

Two kites flying northwards side by side like winged ploughs.

A no-doubt-classic recurring nightmare theme for me and probably for many others: losing one's way.

Arriving at the height of a fashionable reception at P. V.'s house. There are many guests and the crowd keeps growing. There are people everywhere, all upper bourgeoisie and aristocratic types, various settings, monuments among the rocks, a chapel in which a very short man can be seen officiating some service. It's the multiplicity, the abundance that led me astray. The roads descend into ravines. Night approaches such that I am as worried about stumbling as about getting lost. How can I notify and reassure my family?

Later, I'm back in Grenoble, accompanied by my two children but the problem remains: How can we get back to Grignan? There are no taxis (we may have been told why). Finally, having found someone to drive us back, we climb into his car; when the man goes up to his apartment to get something, the car starts and takes us, without a driver, into the labyrinth of streets. We must find a roadmap at all costs. There is a small Jewish bookstore, very old-fashioned; and a kiosk you can poke your head in to request what you want. Then, having passed into a 'real' bookstore, we did not find a single map of the region we wanted, nothing but a map of the city and its exits. In this way, anxiety can build until the moment of waking.

Around half past three in the morning or perhaps later: the shock, at the end of an overcast day, of discovering a bright sky with Orion completely visible, almost frightening. The moon is a very thin, recumbent crescent, its ashen light very visible with a telescope. About an hour later, Sirius appears, twinkling. It's the dog after the hunter. Later still, before dawn, clouds return. It's now much cooler.

SEPTEMBER

Two dreams. The first is one of many centred more or less explicitly on the impossibility of finding the place one is meant to be.

We are travelling with our friends, the Rossiers, and as we usually do with them, are staying in a grand hotel. Already, ordering from the menu seems complicated; you have to note your choice on a form in advance and for some absurd reason I can no longer remember it is not at all obvious. But the real problem comes when we have to return to our rooms. My room is number 11.22. The interior of the hotel becomes increasingly complicated, as if we were lost in one of Piranesi's prisons—but in colour and in a style I characterize at the time as 'Tudor' with turrets, spiral staircases, walkways here and there; old-fashioned panels display the room numbers. I easily find 11.23 and 11.21 but never 11.22. There is a veritable crowd of guests always on the move. I soon find myself in a large parlour, very bright, filled with women as elegant as models, some of whom are lying down, others seated—as if composing a tableau vivant called, for example, 'Luxury and Pleasure': while I continue my search without having understood what was going on in the room. The staff member whom I ask once again where my room is says, 'Behind Navarro,' that is, behind a parlour in which the Navarro series is being shown on television; I cannot find this parlour or any other of the entrances indicated. The hotel's interior finally resembles a giant cathedral with people milling about everywhere, especially in the upper galleries. There, I encounter my sister who, noting that it is eight o'clock, the time dinner is served, becomes worried that she will be too late, and this increases my own anxiety. Then, still in these immense, complicated spaces, I approach a large reception desk, placed not near a wall but at the centre of the hall, and so accessible from both sides. However, on the side I first approach it becomes clear to me, because a large white greyhound is lying at the staff member's feet, that I must address the employee on the other side. This man outlines the path I need to follow very rapidly in a language I finally take to be English; I interrupt him to explain that I can't understand him and that Italian—because this is all taking place in Italy— would be better as long as he speaks slowly; and since I can't think of the Italian word for 'slowly' right away, I say '*despacio*' in Spanish. Obviously, there is nothing I can do here that will not go terribly wrong. The dream must have ended without my ever finding my room.

What, then, is the part of me that feels so lost that it leads me to repeat this kind of dream so often? Is the fear of being caught in a labyrinth without Ariadne's thread or with one that is very tangled or often breaks a fear of death? Or, with less pathos, is it the awareness of some failure, of an innate incapacity to find any solution? In any event, one might think the message of the dream repeating night after night is: 'I am lost, the way out is more and more hidden.'

In another dream, I suddenly saw a large wooden vessel, as sizeable and solid as an ancient galley, flying over our 'cabana' which of course elicited our astonishment but not the slightest fear. After circling above us, it finally landed in an open space, much vaster and emptier than in reality the clearing is where the truffle oaks planted seventeen years ago have taken on the appearance of actual trees. I then find myself standing in front of the machine, opened as ferry cargo decks are for vehicles to disembark: the inside resembles a sitting room panelled in wood with people seated as if on a stage set, perhaps even—I'm no longer sure—wearing clothes in the fashion of the late nineteenth century. They are British. One addresses me very politely, explaining that several of them joined together to build this contraption, each one assuming his or her share of the work; he specified that a woman in a long dress seated 'in the foreground', a bit like a harpist, and who looks to me like she could be Lady Ottoline Morrell (who was an English friend of the novelist Catherine Colomb), was responsible for this or that detail in the planning. Because I had seen the aircraft sway dramatically before landing, I voice the opinion that such a mode of travel must be rather rough on the passengers, which he readily concedes. At this, one of the aeronauts asks me if I had a Brendel to offer them; I reply that to my great regret, all my records are in the house down below and I can hardly go get them. From that moment on, it seems to me that I find them rather intrusive. I can't remember if we finally boarded the vessel ourselves or if they left. But before taking off again, there was another change of scene; the aircraft became a kind of rustic cinema with all of its benches occupied; the person I took for a lady, the woman in the long yellow dress, was walking straight up to an Arab prince, fingers of both hands spread wide at the end of her arms stretched out before her as if to shear his throat under the pretext that he was completely out of place here. A little later, this same young Arab, now seated in the front row, held out from under his burnoose some sort of red and aggressive mechanical puppet who was, in fact, the true little prince; the latter was being asked many questions to test his knowledge; the examiner was perhaps still 'Lady Ottoline', someone, in any case, who had been warned about him and of whom all the others approved; whereupon I took up his defence again, suggesting that had Louis XIV—or some other French king, I can't recall—had been questioned as a child, his answers would not have been any better.

Another dream. In Venice, a large, rather terse woman of a certain age—in the dream I am a rather young man—is giving me a tour of her palazzo. As we exit into a large park, I see before me some kind of fjords with valleys bordered by steep rockfaces; at the very end of one of these, I can even see a glacier; I'm delighted at the idea that, so close to Venice, there are sites of such wilderness. When I return to the sitting room, there are new guests, very distinguished elderly men. Since I don't want to leave without saying good-bye to the hostess, the major-domo leads me to her. I tell him I know him and he agrees. Then, back on the streets in Venice, I realize that I'm not too far from the city centre to get there on foot. I can already glimpse the long arc of the Riva degli Schiavoni; but I am standing in a wasteland with buildings under construction in the background; I gradually become aware that the centre is not so close after all; when I notice children stretched out idly on the stone steps, I am overcome with worry, with the certainty that I will be attacked; one of them does come up to me, throwing at me as if in a game some kind of balls or boxing gloves attached by strings, which he handles skilfully, a game that quickly becomes threatening.

These evenings again, seen from above, a light breeze in the leaves, some of which are beginning to rust, the knotgrass flowers lifting their slender, white clusters, as if effortlessly, the sound of boards, of tools here and there, a bird, barely like a living being, barely more than a leaf, hopping with an apparent sense of elation, the sky milky in the distance, the softness of the air: '*Alles atmet und dankt*'—'everything breathes and gives thanks,' as Rilke wrote.

The puff of wind, too weak for the ear to perceive it, the leaves' trembling—moving like wings—in light that can only be described as golden.

The afternoon light suspended like drops from the leaves that are moving a bit more quickly than yesterday. Rare, distant sounds: cars, dogs.

Strange nocturnal outlines—while the sky with Orion the frail appears like a slate covered with schoolboy drawings:

> Child who are no longer a child; you need
>   not lead me . . .
> I unravelled your hair; I unravelled my life . . .
> Messenger, you say nothing that I did not
>   already know . . .

(Oedipus at Colonus . . .)

> They will soon tear me apart
> They are strangers who only know how to
>   destroy,
> degrade, reduce all to nothing.
> What they will make me say will be meaning-
>   less . . .
>
> You, known better than a fruit,
> Remember only this, yes shouted in chorus
>   . . .

(Hands in the shape of a bowl in order to
receive ...)

OCTOBER

Dream. A young girl-friend is 'condemned', this des-
ignation had, I think, primarily a medical sense but
was transposed into a history of incarceration, from
which a man was helping her escape, a Black man, perhaps, in any case a vigorous man, who was planning
the evasion down to the most minute detail; a barque
had been provided for her—I could see the long boat
with its prow and stern rising to points in a canal or a
kind of low lock; for us—'him' and me—a car and a
wealth of precautions (weapons and 'devices'). All of
it as fuzzy in my memory as it was detailed at the time
of the dream. No doubt he would prevail over me if
we had to compete—I had just seen Mikhalkov's *A
Few Days from the Life of I. I. Oblomov.*

Dream fragment: in the middle of an enormous building similar to a factory, majestic and empty, there is a
large cylindrical well, perhaps of marble, in which I
am to submerge on a rope an object to be conserved,
the way we used to store melons in the coolness of

G. B.'s wells in Gordes; but there is some controversy around this simple gesture, as if it could bring grave consequences. At that point, the space changes into a kind of empty chateau in which I can't find anything that I should have and so I wander around feeling lost and unhappy until it is overtaken by a herd of horses, of which at least one recognizes me, as if I had been its master once, with signs of affection that comfort me; in the horse's company, I approach a high door opening onto an apartment. The door is guarded by a leopard that growls as we draw near then quiets and lets us enter and approach an elderly man—perhaps my grandfather, whom I never knew. This man gives me directions or assigns me a mission.

'*Maria, gestirnte Mutter des Nichts*': all that remains of a dream. It was, strangely, a poem by some 'Brechtian'. I forget how it came about, at the end of what story; but it's not such a bad line of poetry: 'Mary, starry Mother of Nothingness'.

NOVEMBER

November moon, gleaming and frigid, and on the ground, thick bundles of persimmon leaves.

Leopardi's moon: 'What are you doing, moon, there in the sky? tell me what, / silent moon . . . ' How I loved this beginning of a poem, how delighted I am to hear it again tonight, opening paths more profound than those cleared in reality by the light of the actual heavenly body!

Dream. In a village—not at all Grignan—people from outside arrive in small groups but we don't know why. They come as visitors or for a celebration. Yet it soon becomes clear that even if they're not hooligans, they've got bad intentions. They're spoiling for a fight and becoming more and more threatening but in a complete calm. The targets of their threats are either shops with large windows and thus openly visible or a house with big bay windows. I am now in one spot, now in the other, frightened by the complete lack of protection. As I attempt to at least close the shutters of one window, I notice that it is barely attached to the hinges. The most oppressive element of the dream is the quiet omnipresence of threat and the enemy's completely 'banal' appearance.

This nightmare is not one. The motor of hatred turns in all directions, rumbling louder and louder, and this rumbling is revolting.

In the beautiful book Pierre Hadot wrote on Plotinus, I rediscover this philosopher and note a few things:

On light:

> [What the soul sees] is a light that suddenly appeared, complete and self-contained, pure, alone, issuing from itself, so that the spirit where it came from, from the outside or from the inside, and, once it has gone the Spirit says, 'It was inside and yet not inside.' But we should not search for the source of this light. For there is no place of origin there. For it neither comes from nowhere nor goes anywhere; it simply appears or does not appear. That is why we must not chase after it, but calmly wait for it to appear, preparing to contemplate it, as the eye waits for sunrise: the sun emerges over the horizon ('out of the Ocean' the poets say) and presents itself for our contemplation . . . [11]
>
> [. . .]
>
> The sage will take care of his earthly self and will bear it as long as he can as a musician cares for his lyre as long as it is not out of order. If his lyre no longer works, he will change instruments or give up playing. He stops using it because he now has something else to do without it. So he leaves it on the

ground. He no longer gives it a glance and sings without any instrumental accompaniment. And yet, there was a reason he had initially been given this instrument. He played it many times.

Also worth noting, the final lines of Hadot's afterword to second edition:

Yet in my eyes, this 'mysterious', this 'inexpressible', this 'transcendent' are not only to be sought, as Plotinus does, in the direction of original Intelligence, Forms, and Unity, that is to say in a movement of withdrawal in relation to multiplicity and the tangible world, but also, and perhaps much more, in the direction of animate and concrete existence, of the emergence and apparition of visible things. To be sure, I have insisted in this book on the value Plotinus grants the tangible world. That being said, it is in his eyes merely a degraded, inferior reality one should distance oneself from. And yet can we not also perhaps discover the inexpressible, the mysterious, the transcendent, the Absolute in the inexhaustible richness of the present moment and in the contemplation of the most concrete, banal, quotidian, humble, immediate reality? And can we not sense in this reality the ever-present Presence? 'Subtract all things,' Plotinus said. But in a living contradiction, shouldn't one also say: 'Receive all things?'

This is what I have tried to do, it seems to me, every time I could; more precisely, every time that a distant element in what was near me pushed to do so.

DECEMBER

Many dreams last night; unfortunately, however, the essential part has evaporated, since I didn't write it down immediately.

The construction our friend G. C., not without a sense of pride, was showing me on his house, which wasn't his real home but a house right at the centre of the village. It was a space he had ingeniously arranged within the thickness of the walls; once you entered that space it became an enormous room like the inside of a church and I admired the exposed brick walls just as I had some time before admired the walls in Saint Irene Church in Istanbul.

This same process of enlarging and ennobling was repeated in another dream set in the chateau of Grignan in which I was astonished to discover immense rooms, one of which opened like a terrace onto gardens with an enormous fireplace over which hung a portrait of someone bearing as an emblem a long sword with something resembling an ear of wheat engraved on the blade. This caused me to say to the unknown woman accompanying me that these weapons certainly allow this personage to be identified and, therefore, help us understand this architecturally remarkable, luxurious and especially noble part of the chateau; I grew indignant at the sight of groups of visitors passing without taking the slightest interest in him.

More dreams, on a different night. On a street in a large city with much traffic, a small bus stops abruptly in our sight; Michel C. gets off, looking a bit thinner and paler than he is. We understand that he and the other passengers in the bus are returning from the funeral of a son of V.'s—who is not any of their actual children—which some obligation, I no longer remember which, kept us from attending. In the course of our conversation, he confides to us what he has had to do since losing his job: something like gilding pens or other small objects he shows us in a photograph in a magazine. We feel vaguely sad and ashamed for him in this setback.

After this, I find myself carrying on my shoulder a pair of 'feathered skis', a fragile luxury item that I have to protect from any possible impacts because I'm on a sort of open-air escalator with real skiers, one of whom, a young girl, jostles me. The item, painted a vermilion shade of red, is as absurd and ridiculous as certain famous brand gifts; perhaps it, too, was decorated by C.

We then find ourselves in a large room without much furniture, only a round table at the centre. We are with V.'s brother, therefore, the uncle of the supposed deceased, who explains at great length, if not clearly, his nephew's tragedy: drugs, perhaps, we think, not particularly surprised to learn of his problems or his rebellion, given his uncle's very 'Old France' statements and rather military tone.

Another dream. In a mountain village, when leaving my sister's house—she had had difficulties with the peasant who was the landlord—I see that the door to the house where our friends B. are staying is open. I go in and climb the stairs but feel somewhat uncomfortable since it is still very early in the morning and I catch a glimpse through a door left ajar of sheets on a still-occupied bed. I tell myself that A. who is ill must not be rising as early as before. On the other hand, a young person, his daughter—who doesn't resemble his actual daughter in the slightest—has awoken. I ask her how her exams went, not at all sure if my question might be taken badly or not. There is also an old woman in the kitchen, probably her grandmother. I then hear A. state, quite nervously, that they are leaving and need to pack their bags. He, too, is in conflict with the peasant who is renting them his farm; this peasant is also the author of regionalist works. To diffuse the situation, I explain to A. ironically that two 'writers' are unable to live under the same roof. He looks drawn and at one point his lips are covered with saliva which alarms me and might explain his extreme nervousness. He then talks about the books he and the peasant had apparently written together and from which the peasant had drawn considerable profit at his expense.

All of this, fundamentally, is profoundly sad. Later, I see them all leaving, driven by the peasant who is grumbling about them; the image is muddled and they could have left in a trailer with the peasant seated upfront on a tractor, saying something like, 'He can swallow his anger, that one! . . . '

More dreams. An erotic scene, without much interest or detail, in which I join a young woman—a person who in reality is very admirable but for whom I feel no attraction—in bed and soon give up, lacking any initiative. Then I hastily search for a towel in large, tall cabinets bursting with all sorts of linens but all of it old and musty, as the room is as well; at that point, all trace of the woman or of cavorting has disappeared; two old women dressed all in black appear, who seem prematurely aged as my sister-in-law and her friend did well before time, and exchange banal remarks.

This was followed by the first dream I can remember about my grandson. The dream takes places outside in a town that is Grignan, although without any resemblance to it; there is a high peak shaped like an ancient tower built on the edge of a crater; I notice certain spherical, greenish rocks and rockslides of red and ochre stones. We are playing on a wall, probably with model cars, and in perfect accord. Suddenly, alerted by a muffled rumbling like that of an avalanche, I raise my eyes and am alarmed at the sight of a landslide forming on the almost vertical flanks of the tower-shaped peak. Frightened people come out of a row of white houses I had not noticed before; I explain to the child that they are escaping to safety and that, where we are, there's nothing to fear.

Finally, a rustic scene in which peasants and residents of Grignan, including C. the painter and plasterer, are preparing an open-air celebration in front of a large, low house. I point out to C. the striking beauty of the flowers, specifically lavender, in this field, of which several sections are bare as happens where tables have been set up—which are not yet decorated; and I am delighted that he is no less susceptible to the beauty of these flowers than I am. Prelude to a country celebration.

1998

JANUARY

A *dream*, or several interwoven dreams. On the shore of a large lake over which a violent wind that had just picked up is rippling the water towards us in an almost menacing fashion, an unknown friend and I try in vain to recall the name. Then (?) while I'm visiting the cathedral of Lausanne, my attention is drawn to (or the guide has indicated) a kind of pillar, said to be of the Ulamas, installed before the main door and covered with Arab writing that testifies to the passage of Muslims in the region. Suddenly, the course of the dream reverses and leads to an enormous room housing many stands and a group of coffee drinkers, all of them Arab. Then the setting is once again the shore of a lake. André Gide appears on a terrace and he asks an employee of the hotel (where we are probably staying) if he is, in fact, alone and whether anyone is following him; she feels obliged to answer, with an air of regret, that no, he's not alone. He turns and sees Ghéon who has, no doubt, come to monitor his deviations; but he evades Ghéon and we assume he is immediately back on the prowl. Coming upon Gide later, stretched out on the floor of a small shack on the water, I thought that he hadn't yet found his prey. I then notice a couple behind a kind of bar or stall; the guide explains that they are Europeans, probably here to make their livelihood. This guide slightly resembles our fried Soysal from Istanbul. I'm embarrassed not to have any local currency on me. Suddenly, I see Gide again in his fishing shack, this time next to four or five small shirts on hangers which represent as many young boy victims of his desires; and I'd like to know exactly how things go between them . . . After this, my guide leads me to another shack, a simple shelter kept by a young woman; but in it, there's water everywhere and I don't have any wish to risk losing a foot, since it's teeming with small serpents; I don't get out fast enough to avoid being stung, superficially, by one of them.

Water vapour in the soil.

Dream of travelling in a foreign country, perhaps Turkey. I am embarrassed to part of a group at the moment of entering a restaurant or a bed-and-breakfast run by private individuals and I grasp, little by little, what we are going to be served. Above all, I remember my father's action at a certain point when he got up to repair something high up on the wall that was threatening to fall, a shelf or some sort of awning mechanism, and my fear that he would not be able to do it. Then, the fact that before serving the contents of a large, round platter, probably a dessert, the hostess, a strong woman, sits on it several times to make it more flavourful—which, even in the dream, astonishes me to no end and makes me doubt that the dish could be remotely edible.

Trails of phrases about flowers, at night:

> What could these flowers be, I said to
> myself,
> growing sparsely in the earth along the path
> I am following . . .
> These steps that bring me home each day at
> the same time lead me elsewhere
> (to the non-home, to what is the oppo-
> site of home)

> . . . It would have been better to say simply:
> pink bindweed
> sparse
> and myself passing . . .

La Fontaine, 'Against Those with Difficult Tastes':

> Who would not deem this
> an act of enchantment?

La Fontaine is speaking of his own fables but not quite in the way we understand it and would precisely define the magical power of the simplest and most lucid turns of phrase in his writing. His grace has no equal except for Racine's, although Racine's has a darker tone. It must elude foreign readers just as Pushkin's eludes us.

The moon visible in the sky in a nearly warm afternoon, a dangerous warmth in the month of January. Like a fingernail or a paper lantern. A nocturnal visitor astray in daytime. A cherry-blossom petal before the season. Light inside light.

Dream of the thief. I received him at home, that is to say, in a small square room with white walls and little furniture; but, waking in the middle of the night, I see him making a mould of the lock with modelling clay.

This relapse, because that's what it is, forces me to ask him to report to the police. It's only later, outside, that I wonder when looking at his features if he's not Maghreb, which he confirms. I remember that then, when saying goodbye to him, I embraced him since we had become friends, perhaps on the strength of his account of his life story which he told me but I forgot. What I retain from this dream is that I felt compassion for him but I also wanted the Law to be respected.

March weather in early winter. Through the window, as so many times before, perhaps better still because the trees in the hotel's park have been trimmed, I see the trees' shadows thrown delicately on the lawns and the linden trees' shiny branches; this luminosity of the immobile branches since there is not a breath of wind, this frail luminescence, this kind of absolutely peaceful expectancy—as when someone sleeps in broad day-light: the trees' siesta. There is this same luminescence on the summit of Mont Ventoux, the same in the wisps of clouds, the same—if I could see it—on the moon.

The Music Room by Satyajit Ray: one of the most beautiful and melancholy tributes paid to a certain form of beauty as it approaches its end. This way of life, this architecture (a rather mongrel one, incidentally), even this music are all very foreign to us; but the dream of them has inhabited us ever since we learnt to read, ever since the never-forgotten *One Thousand and One Nights*: it is the remote that is nonetheless deep within our hearts; and thanks to the filmmaker's art we feel almost as entranced, as shaken, even, in the end as the increasingly ecstatic rajahs gathered in the music room. Even though the chandeliers are extinguished in the last moments of the movie, nothing can erase the fact that the chandeliers were delicate and brilliant marvels; even though death intrudes brutally in the guise of a black shipwrecked boat, nothing can erase the fact that the master of the palace had seen the dancer inscribe her evermore rapid calligraphy in the air as if her very body were tracing the most beautiful love poem ever dreamt.

La Fontaine, 'The Shepherd and the Sea':

> You want my money, oh
> ladies of the water?

The grace of this plural, we don't know why; for its courtesy and for its chiming. And for the musicality of the closing lines:

The sea promises the sun
and the moon;
Yet beware, ill winds and thieves
will follow soon.

Evening: mountain or blossoming rose, open rose, and frozen.

Cold and rain for the burial of our neighbour, Robert T., who died relatively young of an embolism in the middle of the night. The two trestles that await the coffin, the icy chapel with its doors left open, the increasingly otiose words and rites. The frigidity inside and out.

La Fontaine, again, to lure those fish not inclined to let themselves be caught: 'A pond awaits you, crystal clear . . . '

And that other fable, one of the most beautiful, 'The Dream of a Denizen of Mogul', in which we think, at first, that the word 'Mogul' in the beginning has sparked an extraordinarily free and intimate day-dream in celebration of 'the love of solitude'. Here, too, there is no doubt: because he let slip a confidence related to the most secret recesses of his heart, La Fontaine deepens and expands to an almost infinite degree his innate musicality and approaches Racine who very well could have written this verse: 'I dedicate new sacrifices to it in the desert.' (Besides Chamfort already finds similarities between them in their 'audacities' that appear so natural they are sometimes overlooked.)

Most limpid poet of all:

> Who among us will be the last to delight in
>   the brightness
> of the azure firmament? Can any moment
> at all assure you even of the very next?

Old man's wisdom and later, the wisdom of the '*Scythian philosopher*':

> His happiness consists in
> the beauty of a garden;

and the happiness, again, of running water, of lustral water at the same time as a pause:

> Warm waters, they washed
> the travellers' feet . . .

And to conclude, in the very last fable, 'The Judge, the Hospitaler and the Recluse' ('*How could I find a better ending?*'), for one final time the image of pure water is tied to that of the desert as we understood it then, that is, of reclusion:

> The silt forms a thick cloud, creating
> the opposite effect of the crystal stream.
> My brothers, said the saint, let it settle,
> Then you will see your image.
> To contemplate yourselves best, remain in
> the desert.

Dream. Walking with my long-time companion in a mountain valley, after hesitating over which path to take on our descent to keep from passing too close to an occupied house, we first arrive at the edge of a large, empty basin that also resembles a courtyard or a yard. Stopping there, we find ourselves, a bit embarrassed, in the company of the owners of the house showing their young children this strange thing; indeed, we see round openings all along the uphill wall, evidently intended to fill the basin; but the same openings can be seen in the downhill wall. This causes me to wonder out loud how the basin could be filled and if the water only remains at a low level, below these outlets. A marvellous sun illuminates the scene. Continuing on our way we soon see an enormous edifice of ancient and religious aspect, the images of which have not remained in my memory; I only remember that it elicited more surprise, even enthusiasm, in me than in my companion which disappointed me, if not irritated me somewhat. Having entered as visitors, I showed her a series of wooden armoires, carved in a rustic style, which I found particularly beautiful (even though their number and alignment had no clear meaning). Several indications led me to believe we were in Spain. The place was called Siis (I'm far from certain about this name); it turned out this was a place well-known for, in fact, its strangeness. Farther on there was an immense zoo (its dimensions, as so often in my dreams were extensive); more precisely: animals of very rare species (I don't remember exactly which) were gathered in buildings that were not originally intended for them, outbuildings of a seminary, perhaps, or a convent; a religious building in any case, which explained its age and the beauty of its architecture. Before it, no sense of dread or anxiety, only very vivid surprise and the pleasure of the surprise experienced while travelling on the discovery of a site you hadn't intended to visit.

(The sense of dread, bizarrely and perhaps not for the first time in my life, is deep within me, of the variety experienced the night before an exam or before a vertiginous mountain pass. I can't find any reasonable explanation for it in my immediate environment—either in space or time—aside from the assumption that in my viscera more than in my

head I am sensing death, the symptoms and manifes-
tations of which are naturally multiplying in greater
and greater proximity. If that is the case, is there a
remedy for fear and for the fear of being afraid?)

FEBRUARY

Tonight's dreams. Once more, in my nocturnal life, I
get lost in the suburbs, searching in vain for a taxi;
when I finally find a telephone booth to inform my
mother of my delay, all I hear on the end of the line is
sobbing. Arriving home—along what paths, I don't
know—I enter a dining room I don't recognize that
is almost entirely filled with an abnormally large
square table, set with twenty or so places; my father
is sitting at the table alone. I repeat my apologies, truly
overcome with sadness. Then after a series of forgotten episodes, I catch sight in a large manor house or
maybe a chateau of a young girl dressed all in white,
condemned or threated, who is fleeing as fast as she
can towards a forest. Her father, a man of great poise,
is overcome with fear and, after notifying the police,
leaves to find her. However, the girl has already
returned and is put into my arms—but it's nothing
more than a little, a very little emaciated body, of
which we see many too many these days in the news,
victims of starvation; still dressed in white, reduced to

almost nothing, but alive; and we know that she will be saved. Despite my revulsion, I cover her with kisses.

Trip to Milan.

A derailment in the Milan station changes the schedule. Instead of aggravating me, this delay sharpens my attention. The streets of Brig are resplendent with sunshine, yet they still don't tempt one to linger. Sitting in the train and waiting for it to depart, I try to read Nathalie Sarraute's *Here*, the only 'possible' paperback I found in the station along with one by Quignard; still, as short as it is, I don't finish it (just as, later, I'll drop the *Petits Traités* [Short Treatises] on account of the mannerism that spoils certain pages).

The trip will have three stages: a regular train to cross the Simplon Pass; a regional train covered with tags from Domodossola to Gallarate; and buses to reach Milan.

The large curtains of grey ice among the boulders in the Alps just before the close of day.

After night has fallen:

a woodfire in a garden and lights in the small marble containers in the cemetery walls;

the litany of train stations where we stop constantly, that is, every ten minutes, these names please me almost as much as they did on my first trip more than fifty years ago: Vogogna, Premosello, Cuzzago, Candoglia, Mergozzo;

the pink plaster of these stations, their ragged palms;

then the most prestigious names on the shore of Lake Maggiore: Verbania, Baveno, the palazzo of Isola Bella as pale as an Elsinore, Stresa, Belgirate;

every once in a while, someone enters these more-or-less empty, rocking train cars, people who look poorly, tired, silent; it's getting later and later;

finally, in the car we've crowded into, the same silence, the same tiredness, but no aggression; a man is holding on his lap, not his suitcase as we do but a black animal with horns, which I take to be a little goat until, upon looking more closely, I see it is a dog with bandaged ears.

During my first meal, in the hotel restaurant—it is therefore very late—I hear these few words spoken at my back that charm me even more than the station names, waking so many warm memories: '*Ingegneri, come va?*' and, at the same table a little later, '*Grappa per i signori!*' Facing me, a young woman alone smiles into her mobile phone; at the next table a young man, also alone, immersed in a book next to his plate.

In Brera we are welcomed by the Iesi collection that fills the entire entrance hall; is it my state of vague euphoria that leads me to consider it of rare quality, notably a large Braque (it was a long time since I'd seen a work of his that elicited so much of my admiration as this one)?; small portraits by Modigliani, very dense, and rather old Morandis, dark, intense, almost dramatic, in contrast to the subtle self-portrait of 1924, luminous and contemplative.

Little five- or six-year-old schoolgirls sit cross-legged in front of Veronese's immense *Feast in the House of Simon the Pharisee* with paper and pencils.

Tintoretto's very strange canvas, *Discovery of the Body of Saint Mark*, companion piece to *Saint Mark's Body Brought to Venice* in the Accademia: a scene from an imaginary opera, funereal with those half-height tombs and walls of an Alexandrian portico, a feverish choreography that the saint's gesture is meant to calm and in which the light that swells from under a raised flagstone in the back of the nave is stranger still. There is a line from this painting straight to El Greco then Bacon.

The beauty of Piero della Francesca's altarpiece has an astronomical aspect; due less to the fact that the jewels in the hair of the figures in the background shine like stars than to the silence that reigns over the motionless flow of persons subject to a divine order.

Seen from the train on the way home:

the gasometer and the bare trees, pylons, bridges, rusting shacks, run-down sheds in pitiful little gardens, factory chimneys. A small canal bordering narrow yards, the villas' stingy architecture. Thin shadows scattered over the grass by a weak sun seem to me, not for the first time, the most mysterious utterance. You can feel springtime ready to erupt under the straw of the fields. The snow on the mountains, which we approach before going into the tunnel, is dazzling.

The pastels of Gérald Goy in the museum of Vevey: Goy is exactly the anti-Lélo Fiaux—several of whose feverish and vibrant watercolours hang on the neighbouring walls; these paintings are also touching in that they remind me of the time when I saw them being created. Goy does not leave his home, so to speak, and is more of a magician than any other in that, over time he magically transfigures the small patch of garden he sees from his window. He has no need for any adjacent exterior, nor for any kind of drug. It's the incense of the mundane burning very slowly. Dust become magic. When I look at his best works (and to be sure, it is not necessary for all painting to be reduced to this alchemy), I think of what Rilke wrote about angels as he created them: 'pollen of flowering divinity'; This is truly something like that.

The full moon at the close of day: mostly paid for with this ivory coinage, the day's work, a life's long toil.

Because, having begun reading *L'effacement* [The Erasure] by Jacques Borel, I just listened to the sonatas of Bach and Mozart performed by Leonhardt and Kuijken—more unexpectedly in the case of the second of these two composers—I was struck, transported by what I spontaneously called the *élan*, the leaps of the 'spiritual stag' (an expression that, in retrospect, only half-pleased me), these rather unexpected words occurred to me with regard to Borel: 'a man of little faith.' It was a spontaneous, uncontrolled reaction to the first pages of the book in a section titled 'Losing'. Borel writes of his horror of all those who want to win, to win at all costs, contrasting them to the figure of Kleist, pulling his lover into the vertigo of their double suicide. Reading these lines without forgetting the profundity with which they were proclaimed, albeit not to anyone, I thought it absurd to take Kleist as a model—as if, by the way, he hadn't lost for having first wanted, frenetically, to win too much; and that in the end it wasn't a matter, for us, of wanting to lose or to win, but of choosing a measure outside these categories. For a long time that is what separated me from a writer I had always felt close to and who shared many of my most ardent admirations. Knowing this today, still, in listening to Bach or Mozart (whom he mentions in this very chapter and on this very topic), all my doubts dissipated; yet I remained incapable, nonetheless, of turning them into clear certainties.

I continued to leaf through this slender book as if it were by someone very close to me, confronting the same questions as I, using the same recourses against dread in the face of death, of the unknown. Except that in his work negativity is more invasive and ready, at almost every instant, to overcome him. (It could be that this is solely attributable to the difference in our lives, his infinitely more troubled than mine.)

As I continued my reading, I came upon this 'echoing Guillevic': 'The bowl and these same vanished mouths in it, always drinking.' It answered what I had thought with regard to losing and winning: that this is not what is necessary, wanting to lose or wanting to win; rather, far removed from any thought of loss or gain, welcoming, gathering.

Recalling one of the sonnets to Orpheus in which Rilke wrote 'Song is Being', he notes: 'Has this lengthy, this trembling hope lingered in me long enough—or, since childhood, its inane gamble, its vanity?'

That is the central question: Can poetry thus extended, but also painting and music (for example, Chardin and Mozart, whom he compares so aptly in this same book), still be for us a 'trembling hope' (the hope that there is a profound link between 'song' and 'being' if, indeed, they are not one and the same, that is to say, that works express meaning, however we understand it; or, in other words, that the fullness they lavish upon us is not a decoy)?; or do they constitute nothing more than an 'inane gamble'—and the harshness of the word 'inane' would then betray the bitterness of an ardent passion disillusioned.

We do not depart from this inquiry when we read a bit later: 'It was the sea long ago that carried away the sandcastles—and for whom now, for what, less solid than before, rebuild them?' No doubt, no doubt . . . but I remember having written very long ago in a poem about a 'pussy-willows': 'No matter that they crumble into dust if they shine', if they shone for a few days, in March; not allowing the shadow of death to spread over what came before.

My mother, my daughter, nailed to the same childhood, and it is as if, twinned, merged, the same smile above the same tile floated in the air, at the window as before, and this lost bird trill quivers and trembles.

The most painful deaths, one too slow, the other too abrupt, and the remembered smile, and the bird singing beyond the windows, that is what the words are able, after all, to connect (and one thinks of Schubert, in less fluid); as, elsewhere in the book, the almost eternal rose which one refuses to believe is only a phantom . . .

Scarves, shawls of mist in the gardens which a guest, an invisible passenger could wrap herself in when the evening grows cool. A scarf draped over the shoulders of night or of the silence to come.

Those Byzantine churches in Armenia, in Georgia, in Cappadocia as two books allow me to discover them: *L'art arménien* [Armenian Art] and *Byzance médiévale* [Medieval Byzantium]; one is captivated, profoundly (by simple photographs), but what is the source of the captivation? And the thought occurs that *nothing more* in all contemporary art will hold its own next to this (right or wrong, this is the thought that comes). I also think that, of the very few trips I would still want to risk taking, this would be the most tempting. Why?

I remember my exultation before Sant' Antimo in the wheat fields south of Siena (and many other churches I have visited, without faith, in my life); is it the same thing? There is some of the same and something other.

The same is the presence in and around it of something sacred that seems to pulsate there still like a very weak but unmistakable flame.

The other could be their location, on *boundaries*, in the desert, in the mountains. Like watch towers, or defences, or outposts: a word addressed where the danger is greatest.

Raised stones amid sparse gravel.

(A leafy rinceau, finely arched is enough to indicate that these are not simply casemates or covered wells or pylons.)

Massive, compact: the better to protect their invisible core. As if they had been built in the image of the mountains that surround, that overhang them. Enceintes of their embryonic gods.

Bach's violin and piano sonatas: a source of exultation today as much as the first time when our friend André Wachsmuth-Loew played one or two in the organ gallery of Grignan. I think of crowns, of a quiet coronation, of the motionless angels in Piero della Francesca's *Baptism of Christ*: free order, the open temple, wide open. Also of something that unfolds and folds like a large white wing.

If you then listen immediately to the sonata Mozart wrote for the same instruments (in this case, K. 376), what is most striking is the triumphant youthfulness, an almost impudent lightness and agility, a bird's movement. Besides, the bird-catcher is not far; it's in the third movement, you think you hear his laughter: Ariel in Vienna. It's true that up there, the air is so pure, so iridescent that we would be tempted to laugh, as a child laughs or a fairy. Laughter without shadow.

Dreams. In the first I see de Gaulle take his photograph from the wall in a nearly empty white room in a large house that looks more like a villa than any chateau or official building. I freely tell him my regret at seeing him resign, as if we were close friends. He calmly answers in the same tone with no trace of emotion or grandiloquence that he has made his decision and it is final.

In the second, on the road I'm driving on—a national road or even a highway—I am surprised to notice an abrupt slowing of traffic. It is due to people from the Front National. Here and there are drivers on the verges, their feet bound in chains, two by two. Then the scene changes; now we are all on foot, waiting rather tensely, restrained by members of the FN, not at all kindly but still watched over by several polices officers so that the situation does not degenerate. The situation gradually improves, the tension lowers; but not without everyone feeling great astonishment and deep worry about what these people are capable of and the sluggishness with which they are fought.

Violets: the surprise, their suddenness when moving a stack of wood that was hiding them. A pale colour with a bit of white, very small, in groups. When finding them, a true joy, a bit like a child finding an Easter egg, but different because I wasn't looking for anything at the time. And yet, how tiny they are, frail, wan, almost insignificant! Will I be able to do them justice one day? In the light, itself fragile as well, of early spring.

A walk on Montagne des Ventes, above Comps. The first green of the fields between the hedges. The church is built of a stone scarcely less green; it looks like a barn or else like a squat lighthouse. Marking a centre in the place of hills, a mean.

In the valley, the Lez's sinuous waters shine in the polished rock like light that has already cleaved the rocks. The true path, coolest and without blemish.

Dream. I go to a chateau that is the residence of an important English lord, a hero of a Shakespearean play, whom I am supposed to meet. I am both in the reality that inspired this play and on its stage set. On my tour of the chateau, I notice a group of students around a table in a pergola participating in one of Bonnefoy's seminars with Bonnefoy himself seated at the head of the table; the seminar is evidently devoted to this play; it's Bonnefoy who tells me the king's name: Richard VI. To his right is seated a female student whom, it seems to me, he treats with great solicitude, perhaps because she's very ignorant or a bit vacuous, and to whom he has to explain everything. I'm probably somewhat jealous. Later, Yves B. and I must get in a barque to follow a canal dug inside the chateau, probably in order to visit the king I was searching for at the beginning of the dream; it's a black boat with two pointed ends, like the crescent of a moon that has set; as we are embarking, I point out to B. that the barque, since it's 'of the period', risks being worm-eaten and we could sink with it in this canal in which the water flows quite impetuously.

The flowers: it's as if, with the passage of time, I were moving from relatively prestigious flowers—peonies, primroses—to other, more and more humble flowers, blooming at ground level: like the bindweed in the fields. I sensed in advance that I'd never be able to express their hidden 'truth', that they defy poetry and so on, knowing all too well what would be repeated about them yet again in a fated cycle.

JUNE

At the entrance of the first of the Louvre's new Egyptian rooms stand admirable and mysterious bronze 'palettes': before we know anything about them, their use, their meaning. Like signs erected at the beginning of a path—dark, almost mute, their power intact. Any artist today who would try to imitate them with a futile return to the past would produce only a void.

❦

Dream, from which I've retained only a few images simultaneously intense and vague. A woman, completely unknown to me who has been interned several times—in a prison, perhaps, or in a lunatic asylum—is sitting next to me in steep terrain in which the sea might be visible in the distance; closer, at our feet, there is someone, no doubt a peasant in his field or his garden; I therefore dissuade her from escaping in that direction since she would be denounced right away —from this I gather that I saw her at that moment rather as a prisoner. Later, I come upon her again in an enormous room or courtyard of an asylum this time but it's a man, obviously lost. I talk to him; and since he tells me he knows Hingis well ('The cousin of the tennis champion,' I say, which he confirms), I assure him that his situation will be resolved, the aforementioned Hingis being an influential politician—that is, I suppose he will be freed. Then I wake up.

It's four thirty in the morning; a brilliant crescent moon emerges from the black trees and I can hear the very first birds of the morning. I listen to them attentively for a long time, marvelling all the while at this passage from one plane to another, as if through a non-existent door. Initially, for a long time, they are weak and brief, shy, separated by rather long silences. They resemble calls, timid shades looking for each other, travellers about to set out on their journey, meagre souls in distress. Then, in a very slow progression, these calls grow longer, more frequent, a bit more resonant: tests of rhythms, as a poet of old might have tried different verse forms or feet, iambs, dactyls, trochees; also a bit like an orchestra tuning, its members invisible. In any case, it is a beginning, at first seeming fearful, or at least prudent; these are first steps. Not yet song; but after a certain time, phrases that are more or less musical have formed nonetheless, flute lines. The word 'twittering' would suit these beginnings well.

At the same time, I feel overcome with an almost adolescent discomfiture, a sensual languor, as if the old man found himself removed far back in his life, enveloped in the reverie at the end of nights that were too solitary.

(It was only an old man awake well before dawn, whom the moon and the birds helped emerge from his nightmares.)

So then, added to what dream contributed, what the outdoors and my personal state contributed, were memories of my reading. Having looked at the clock, I first thought of some lines by Rimbaud (my edition of *A Season in Hell* is dated 1942):

At four in the morning, in summer,
The sleep of love endures.

and of the '*workmen*' he mentions later, the '*carpenters in shirt sleeves*'. Then, noticing that this other text, one of the poetic fragments that had pierced my heart the first time I read it and I never forgot, was an almost literal translation of what I had just heard, I remembered the passage on dawn in Claudel's *Tête d'or* [Golden Head], I'd bought the edition the same year, 1942:

> The frigid violet morning
> Glides over the distant plains, tinting each
>   rut with its magic!
> And in the silent farms, the roosters call:
> Cock-a-doodle-doo!
> It's the hour when the traveller, huddled in
>   his car,
> Wakes and, peering outside, coughs and
>   sighs,
> And the newborn souls, along the walls and
>   forests,
> Uttering weak cries like naked newly
>   hatched birds,
> Fly away again, guided by meteors, into
>   regions of obscurity . . .

(In this way another door opened slightly onto the region of books read; and all this was mingled in my confused, but attentive mind.)

Dream. Several young people, of whom I was one, were facing problems choosing their careers, their lives; less than a question of profession, in fact, it's a question of mission, of vocation, of noble, serious and generous intentions. One of these young people, whom I don't know, seems to be intent on gaining my friendship; to the point where I feel obligated, somewhat against my inclination, to follow the same path (I don't know which) so as not to distress him.

'Later', I am welcomed into an Indian community, Southeast Indian, by a solemn old woman, responsible for instructing me; I find myself in an Indian dress and one important element of the ceremony consists of engraving characters on each of my toes; the young girl in charge of this tells me it might cause some pain, like branding. It does, in fact. After this I find myself walking through a large city filled with passers-by; I enter a stand in which, unable to speak the language, I have the feeling they are taking advantage of me. Then I enter other unfamiliar places that may be dangerous. Later, I meet a French actor who is performing there in an outdoor theatre at the foot of the great walls in the centre of the city; I can't remember what he says to me until I notice Samuel Beckett standing next to me, very straight, his manner as demanding as ever; as a result I am more and more ashamed of my ridiculous disguise, unjustified as it is. At some point in his pronouncements—he talks at length—he is severely critical of Claudel whose lecture at the Vatican had been well-received because he had carefully avoided mentioning the problem of the poor . . . Of the poor, two appeared on the side of the road, vagrants who called to me and fought bitterly over a bottle of wine.

Night. A swarm of stars, all the more striking for being framed, bordered, or crossed by vaguely luminous clouds. The words '*jeune fille*' [young girl] occur to me because of the rhyme with '*brille*' [shine] but not only because of that.

Something you find again accidentally and that won't trouble you. The hive. You are ageless in the face of it. Or you imagine you are.

SEPTEMBER

Looking at the trees, the other evening, completely black against the sunset sky, I remembered a line from a poem probably written in 1943—'The birds flew down towards the earth's heart'; first because some birds few past, no doubt returning to their nests; and also because later in the poem are the lines: 'The sky has lost its lustre on the low house / And, under the slender trees fencing off the horizon . . . '; that is to say, I was touched by exactly the same thing, albeit with the rather significant difference that I had at the time associated it with a state of amorous melancholy I no longer feel today, fifty-five years later. What consoled me—for the passage of time—is that, after all, with age, up to a certain point at least, your powers of expression improve. You no longer say just anything, you are less enchanted with words; and with more modesty, you go further or become more profound. Writing of these birds that they 'slide towards the soporific silence of love,' what nonsense, what vain, hollow music! Paris, friends from Paris, were a great help in my effort to shed these ready-made inflections and this dubious vagueness. Even if I was never entirely cured of that 'melodiousness' which my most ardent admirations infused in me: Baudelaire, Mallarmé, Verlaine—even Claudel.

It is nevertheless true that these trees, suddenly turned black, could evoke a fence forged of a material more pliable than iron or dark lace against a sky the colour of skin; but, as always, it was not so easy to transpose it. It was as if the night had invaded, infused these plants before all the rest, as if it had drawn in charcoal on a still luminous sky a moment before fusing with it. Drawing in charcoal, in coal, in lines of soot. And, indeed, familiar birds descend from the heavens where they had been enjoying themselves during the day, in a confident and oblique flight, behind these fences of a sort, towards their nests, and it's like the trace of a phrase nearing its end, a felicitous, soothing conclusion to the day's labours. All we would need to do is follow their example. Only a dormouse or two would be left, leaping with a kind of malice like acrobats just as black as their delicate springboards; and later, perhaps, the increasingly white mirror of the moon opposite, to reflect worry or pleasure.

Children playing knucklebones with their ancestors' remains: 'thoughts' between sleep and waking. More images of frail, hollow things. Dice or dominoes of death. Foetus. Bodies emptied of their substance. The refusal to think of it, to think of what awaits you, the flight from it. Yet a kind of trembling that comes over you unexpectedly, a faint, discreet, vague, hidden fear, more in the legs than the head (we think).

Masses of greenery, masses of clouds; disorder in the sky, apparently, at least.

The effect of surprise is so important: I remember, this year in the spring, the first clumps of violets in the garden that dazzled me but from which, a few days later, I'd already let the light escape. Why?

Interrogating a clump of violets discovered while moving wood. It's as if a very hunched man were reading a book close to the ground. Apparitions. This is what nourishes poetry: first fruits. Because of them there is less repetition, even though poetry always says more or less the same thing.

Consequently, in the book by Kenji Miyazawa, the Japanese poet who died in 1933 at the age of thirty-seven, I read the lines addressed to his sister from his deathbed:

> In your harsh, harsh fever, panting,
> you asked me
> for a last bowl of snow
> that fell from the sky,
>   the world called galaxy . . . [12]

and these from the following poem:

> [you] ask me to go with you . . .
> your cheeks however
> how beautiful they are.

I'll put these fresh pine boughs
on top of the mosquito net
they may drip a little . . . [11]

Maybe everything is there or almost everything; a few 'thoughts under the clouds' without the excessive eloquence of my poems; a few gestures to cool the sweat just before death.

Debussy sung by Mary Teyte led me to reopen Tristan l'Hermite's *The Promenade of the Two Lovers*, with titles so close to Couperin's:

Would you, with sweet privilege
Place me above humankind?
Let me drink from your cupped hands
If the water does not melt their snow.

Here, too, we see preciousness brush up against the marvellous in places; and more often simply wittiness.

The dreams of slumbering water . . .

OCTOBER

All these dreams of getting lost: are they telling a truth, that is, that deep inside, we are truly lost and not happy but anxious that we are? Most often, we experience an anxiety that does not stop growing until the dream is interrupted when we wake because time is passing and the chances that we will find the place or goal we seek—home, hotel, refuge—decrease accordingly. In a recent nightmare of this kind, I was calling Michel Rossier in a voice that certainly didn't carry far enough and was growing hoarse; in others, it's the telephone that is not answered or the line is cut. We call for help, we are alone, night is falling. We see what this prefigures.

The wind, which has returned with the sun, chases the first yellow leaves through the transparent air; this reminds me of the thousands of fireflies in Tenuta di Ricavo the other summer or of a burst of sparks. Then, in an instant, everything is extinguished under a cloud.

Foliage as brilliant as the surface of a rippled lake in full sun. Rarely has Mont Ventoux looked so much like a dog lying on the threshold of a garden.

The light trembling, as if just before an impending ordeal, a vague, muted fear or something like that. From below.

Sicily

In the small propeller plane taking us to Milan, I happen on photographs in the *Alitalia* journal of Ninfa, the Caetani's property where I stopped in 1949—the promised 'oasis'; I only vaguely recognize the site, but this reminder of a trip from so long ago after my discovery of Sicily does not leave me indifferent. Improvising a thank-you speech for the Mondello prize, I'll speak of the 'waters' voice' I had heard in that garden back then, I'll call it 'angelic' in an era bereft of angels with the distinct impression that the adjective will not be understood.

Our room in the President Hotel, facing the port but separated from the sea by an eight-lane road, noisy and full of pollution from morning to night, a very ordinary room with a window looking onto a part of the city that had been bombed in previous times: sheds covered with sheet metal and a few scattered tiles, courtyards of garages in which dogs roam—one of them will try to bite my ankle one morning when I pass by in an attempt to avoid the infernal traffic along the sea; farther off, only mediocre rental buildings are visible and beyond them, higher up, a cirque of bare hills that look very much like our mountains with a much more rugged relief.

One morning, awake at six, I see the dawn light between pink and yellow which makes this setting almost beautiful; around seven, some young people come out of a shed. A corpulent woman in a blouse, her arms very tan, appears on the terrace of a squalid brick house. In a building hardly less run down, three superimposed scenes of waking remind me of Hopper's bleak paintings. There is still very little noise; the light is dusty.

Rising like a ghost in the middle of this setting, a four-storey building with a mouldy white roughcast exterior and downpipes clearly visible between the windows, several of which are half-blocked with rubble or sandbags as if we were still in middle of the conflict. Some of the 'apartments', if that word can be used for them, are empty. At least three are occupied, those on the ground floor with barred windows, all of them with long curtains hanging on the balcony railings. One night, having trouble sleeping, I would look for a long time at a room on the top floor, still vaguely illuminated, more or less protected from the rain by long plastic curtains billowing in the strong gusts of wind, trying in vain to someone moving in it. A fitting scene for a 'Ghost Sonata' of our time.

At the very formal prize ceremony in the city hall, during which the mayor, Orlando, will speak of his city with courage and intelligence, the laureates are seated facing the jury as if for an exam. I feel out of place. Poetry is a thousand miles from such displays. I prefer to think of the large ochre mass of the cathedral in

Cefalù under a very grey sky and its small port lashed by aggressive waves. Or of the two faces we admired in the Palazzo Abatelli: that of da Messina's *Virgin Annunciate*, who has just heard the angel of the Annunciation, and the other, sculpted by Laurana, as pure as a Brancusi, the 'soul' in addition—dare one say.

Is it just my fatigue, my aggravation at being mixed up in these literary ceremonies, trying awkwardly if not impolitely to steal away, and the wear and tear of age that have prevented me from enjoying Italy this time as before? Perhaps. But it could also be that the beauty of, among other things, certain churches like the bare chapel of the Chevaliers du Saint-Sépulcre, is something that is becoming increasingly distant from us, not only because we have seen so much of it or because our gaze has become blunted but also for what made it meaningful is shrinking, waning—for us; which leads you to wonder what you're doing here, hunting ancient emotions in places that are almost empty the way you would try to warm yourself at a hearth filled with cold ashes.

In a tiny stand next to the Oratory of the Rosary of Saint Dominic—where we were not able to muster enthusiasm for Serpotta's stuccos and their tired Baroquism—a stand feebly lit even though it was closed, we noticed shiny metal ex-votos, statuettes of saints being restored and a large dog lying down and an enormous long-haired black cat. It's the elderly guardian of the oratory who still comes to work in her four square metres after decades. May the saint who is about to be celebrated protect her! Night and the rain are imminent.

What creaks and stiffens more and more often in the body, the joints; the effort it takes to remain straight.

Always these flights of yellow birds that are leaves torn from the trees by the north wind. Trees that vibrate, that shine rather than tremble. Of their thousands of leaves. The liveliness of things at the mercy of the wind. With no connection to any human emotion whatsoever—not fear, joy, or fever. Close, certainly, to the sparkling of waves in the sun. The multiplicity, the movement, a quivering neither fearful, nor happy. (Still, more happy than frightened or tormented.) The scintillation. Gentle sparks. And the pale clouds traveling overhead, asleep.

Hopkins (1844–89). Again, I leaf through the precious book published in the 10/18 series. *Carnets-journal-lettres* [Notebooks–journal–letters]. The quasi-scientific precision of his observations, especially of water, recalls Leonardo's drawings, the stream: 'Glazed water o'er a drowsy stone.'

On 18 May 1870, he writes:

> One day when the bluebells were in bloom, I wrote the following. I do not think I have ever seen anything more beautiful than the bluebell I have been looking at. I know the beauty of our Lord by it.

Later, returning to the bluebells, he emphasizes 'the Greek rightness of their beauty,' the glare of the light that emanates from them.

Nightmare. The other night, I'm unable to reach Venice, lost as I am in squalid suburbs without any hope of finding a taxi. And last night, a conflict in 'Bulgaria' ('I hate Bulgarians,' I shouted at one point, harassed by their police); a tall man dressed in black who was threatening us with a weapon in the back of a depot—we, that is a small group of strangers subject to his threats, without my understanding exactly why. As if we were resisters or spies. We live cowering under beds or running through the streets exposed to gunshots that could come from any direction. Sometimes we wear masks. There's also a woman with us who does not remind me of anyone I know. Once we have finally escaped the menace, an emotionally vivid scene follows as we are dispersing, happy to be safe but sad to be parting. I see myself tearfully hugging someone still wearing his mask—as if the dangers we ran had cemented an intense friendship between us.

Do not forget: these colours in the landscape seen on my return from the Val des Nymphes at the very end of the day; colours as are rarely seen, seeming transparent at first glance; colours like one more mystery on the horizon.

Like extremely thin layers, layers of glazing that let something luminous pass through from below; translucent without gleaming.

Glass slides, scales no doubt. But why, in the end, did it hold my gaze, touch a chord deep inside me?

I'll have to come back to this one day, if the fear of excessive rumination doesn't prevent me.

'The flowers' encounter.'

Fundamentally, it's the same question I've been asking myself since my eyes were first opened to the outside world as 'nature', that is, since I've been living here: the experience that a particular moment in the day, an element of nature, a river, rocks, an orchard—and more intensely in the past few years, a few flowers—is 'one of the most beautiful things I've ever seen.' What could this mean? Or is it without any meaning? Or perhaps beyond all meaning that we can grasp?

Such questions don't seem to have occurred to me very often (but I may be mistaken out of sheer ignorance). The Greeks didn't discuss nature very much. A flower served merely to highlight a woman's beauty, for example. And if Plato had observed one, it would very likely have been to see in it sparse, inferior forms of supreme Beauty, a stage one must pass through to reach Beauty. For a long time, flowers will be around to express something other than themselves; painters scatter them on the dresses of nymphs and goddesses. They are not wrong to pair up these two graces; but there's something else, something the poets of haiku may have felt and suggested better than the others *by not saying it*. This intuition (in which idea, feeling, emotion and memory are perhaps inextricably intertwined) has become an insistent one for me (not unlike a secret counsellor constantly trying to instil something in my mind by whispering in my ear without my having managed to understand the point, if there is one); this intuition truly has become a central one. I have found a close equivalent only in Senancour (an illuminating one in the lines I quoted in *Landscape with Absent Figures*), though I'd also told myself that I'd have a greater chance of finding others in Novalis' fragments or Joubert's notebooks than elsewhere. These are rather kindred spirits and not only by virtue of the period in which they lived.

It's high time I clarified my thoughts on this and that I draw—who knows?—some kind of support.

The swiftness of these days, as if they truly were fleeing, escaping us. Still, it's not that we get nothing out of them. Like horses escaping the coachman? It's the first image that comes to mind but it's false. This is not a case of recklessness, of brutality.

Birds and leaves carried off in the same direction by the violent, relentless wind. As if they came from the same hearth. And like the days.

As if these were fleeing more and more quickly even. Like water draining from a bathtub, irresistibly drawn down. Does this impression come from what the days lose of their reality, their flavour, as they dwindle? Perhaps. Then everything will end with a story of spectres who retain nothing more in their hands than the shadows of things.

But this is still too beautiful. Because in the end we are not swept away as easily as leaves.

All the pinks, all the roses of winter, clouds, foliage and smoke, blooming in the cold as the sun prepares to sink beneath the horizon. Burning relays handed on. A sceptre passed from hand to hand, furtively, perhaps just a baton enflamed by the pink of evening. Do not let go of it too soon.

NOTES

1 A reference to the French translation by Jaccottet, *Rastelli raconte*, which was published in 1987. [Trans.]

2 Unless otherwise mentioned, all translations of the French and German quotations are by me—[Trans.].

3 Victor Segalen's account of an imaginary expedition from Peking to Tibet; it was published in 1929. His collection of prose and poems, *Stèles*, first appeared in a French–Chinese bilingual edition in 1914. [Trans.]

4 Marcel Proust, *Remembrance of Things Past*, VOL. 1 (C. K. Montcrieff and Terrence Kilmartin trans) (New York: Random House, 1981), p. 381. [Trans.]

5 Martin Buber, *Ecstatic Confessions*: *The Heart of Mysticism* (Esther Cameron trans.) (Syracuse, NY: Syracuse University Press, 1996), p. 43. [Trans.]

6 I was not aware then that the temple of Segesta was never finished; however, this does not alter my observations.

7 See note 'September 1969' in *Seedtime* [In English: *Seedtime*: *Notebooks, 1954–1979* (Tess Lewis trans.) (London: Seagull Books, 2013), pp. 168–71.].

8 See Henry David Thoreau, *Walden; or Life in the Woods* (Boston, MA: Boston, Ticknor and Fields, 1854), p. 98. Subsequent quotations are from the same edition, pp. 106 and 332. [Trans.]

9   A reference to David Mus' rendition of P. B. Shelley's verse: 'O Wind, / If Winter comes, can Spring be far behind?' [Trans.]

10 See Pierre Hadot, *Plotinus or the Simplicity of Vision* (Michael Chase trans.) (Chicago, IL: University of Chicago Press, 1993), p. 61. Subsequent quotations are from the same edition, pp. 102 and 113. [Trans.]

11 Kenji Miyazawa, *Selections* (Hiroaki Sato trans.) (Berkeley, CA: University of California Press, 2007), p. 82. [Trans.]

12 Miyazawa, *Selections*, p. 85. [Trans.]